Growing in Wisdom: A Bible Study in Proverbs for Fathers and Sons

Copyright © 2014 by Dr. Ron Allchin, D.Min.

Published by Biblical Counseling Center Press

Biblical Counseling Center

3233 N. Arlington Heights Road, Suite 302

Arlington Heights, IL 60004

www.biblicalcounselingcenter.org

Cover design by Lucy Ann Moll

Cover photo by iStock

Formerly published in 1994 under the title Ripening Sonship: A Wise Father's Counsel to His Son.

Printed by CreateSpace, An Amazon.com Company

ISBN-13: 978-1499317879

ISBN-10: 1499317875

Growing in Wisdom

A Bible Study in Proverbs for Fathers and Sons

Dr. Ron Allchin, D.Min.

Biblical Counseling Center Press, Arlington Heights, Illinois

Dedicated to

August & May Allchin
My parents whose instruction and teaching have helped guide my life.
Proverbs 1:8

Sherry
My wife who is "a woman who fears the Lord," and is praised by her children and husband.
Proverbs 31:28,30

Christina
My daughter who has "done virtuously."
Proverbs 31:29

Ron, Jr., and Timothy
My sons who have already made "my heart glad."
Proverbs 27:11

Michael
And to all "my sons" in the faith who have allowed me to have a part in their lives.
Proverbs 17:17

A very special thank you goes to all those who have helped make this book a reality.
Thank you to those who typed, proofread, and worked on the many details to produce a book.
You are all special friends!
Proverbs 18:24

Contents

The fear of the LORD

is the beginning of knowledge;

fools despise wisdom and instruction.

Proverbs 1:7

What Is Biblical Counseling Center?

Since 1989, the mission of **Biblical Counseling Center** is "Helping Churches Care for People" by connecting them to Christ's sufficient work and the wisdom of his Word.

We counsel.

We train.

We help.

We serve churches through helping their people receive compassionate, biblical counseling and by equipping their own people to care through counseling training and resources.

Stop by our website: BiblicalCounselingCenter.org

Visit our Facebook page: Biblical Counseling Center

Follow us on Twitter: biblical_cc

Call us: 847-398-7193

Introduction

During my forty-plus years as a pastor and biblical counselor, I've observed the digression of our youth culture. Drugs, teenage pregnancy, alcohol, rebellion toward authority, evil companionship, and all human evil among teens have a common root: **the rejection of wisdom because they did not choose to fear the LORD.**

Dr. Ron Allchin, D. Min.

Parents, pastors, and caring Christians want teen boys to grow in wisdom and become quality sons. But how? I know of few resources available to help teens become quality sons and Christian servants that God and their parents desire them to be. The reason I wrote this book (formerly titled *Ripening Sonship*) is to fill this void and have a resource that helps sons **grow in wisdom.**

The book of Proverbs in our textbook for wisdom.

Proverbs was written from the perspective of a father counseling his son, so these chapters have the viewpoint of a dad speaking to and counseling his son concerning **practical, successful, every day, godly living**. Ideally a father will complete this interactive Bible study with his son. This interaction is important: Did you know two separate studies -- one by the University of Michigan, the other by Penn State University -- stated that the average American dad spends *seven to eleven minutes* of meaningful conversation with each of his children *each week*?

What if a son's father is not available to participate in *Growing in Wisdom*? A father surrogate -- a grandfather, a male youth leader, a friend's father, or a mom -- may fill the "father" role.

It is my desire that dads and sons interact with each other during each chapter. The chapters are designed to not only lead the son into a godly meaningful life and to **strengthen the father in his spiritual life**, but also to maintain and build deeper and more meaningful relationships between fathers and their sons. **Remember, Dad, you're a son too!**

I first used this book among eighth graders in a Christian school to "test" it. Would it make a difference in father-son relationships? Would the dads and boys experience Proverbs in fresh, life-changing ways? Would they grow in wisdom?

Yes! Listen to a few of the stories.

One of the boys and his father had negligible communication before this father-son Bible study. The mother actually did the first several chapters with the son. Not until Chapter 6 on honoring your parents did the boy attempt to involve the father. When he went to his dad with the list "Ways You Can Show Love to Your Father," the dad began to interact with his son. From that chapter on, **the father-son relationship began to grow from a heart made tender by God.**

In another family, the parents were in a bitter divorce battle. The son had alienated himself from his father and had sided with his mother. I suggested to the mother that she send a letter to the father enlisting his support in this father-son study. The father and son agreed to work together on the material three times weekly. It would be great to say the father became a believer in Jesus but this was not the case. However, **their relationship significantly improved during their study.**

Another boy came from a home in which the father deserted the family shortly after his birth. It was agreed that his grandfather would work through this book when available. When the grandfather wasn't available, the mother and son would studied these chapters together. She reported **a tremendous improvement is his attitude toward spiritual things and a significant improvement in their relationship.**

My sons and I also worked through these chapters together. Each evening we would spend time together reading Bible verses and discussing our discoveries. Our relationships grew, and while they're now adults, we regularly reflect on the truth discussed decades ago.

To see fathers and sons grow in wisdom and the fear of the LORD has been rewarding. But perhaps my greatest joy is the personal benefit to my own family and especially my relationships with my sons. **May you experience a deeper, more meaningful relationship with your son as he grows in wisdom.**

I'd love to hear **your personal stories** resulting from working through *Growing in Wisdom*. Please contact me through <u>Biblical Counseling Center</u>. Thank you.

How to Use This Book

Growing in Wisdom: A Bible Study in Proverbs for Fathers and Sons may be used individually or in a group setting, such as a father-son Bible study or small group, a youth group, or in a Christian school classroom.

While it's meant for fathers and sons, others may step in for the dad if he's unavailable. In the Introduction, you read three stories in which moms and a grandfather took the dad's place. Encourage the father to fulfill his responsibility to teach wisdom to his son. When this is not possible, a mom, Christian adult male family member, or a mentor may fill the father's role.

For Individual Father-Son Duos

1. Set aside a specific time and day to work on each chapter. Keep your appointment!

2. Please do no more than one chapter in a sitting. Allow time for absorption, interaction, and application.

3. Look up all verse references in order. Use a pen and notebook to write your answers; or, use your device's note-taking features to type your answers.

4. Complete all Father-Son Interaction Activities.

5. Memorize all assigned verses together and quiz each other.

6. Plan a completion celebration that both the father and son would enjoy. Ideas: a dinner out together, a camp out, or other fun activity.

For Father-Son Bible Studies and Small Groups

One father acts as the leader for a chapter; the responsibility to lead could be assigned to a different father each chapter.

1. Complete 2 and 3 above during the group time.

2. Finish 4 and 5 at home.

3. Plan 6 as a group and have fun.

For Youth Groups, Sunday School Classes, and Classrooms

1. Teach the material to adolescent boys after enlisting the cooperation of each boys' fathers (or mother or guardian if there's no father available).

2. Review the material with at home, both father and son.

3. Complete activities as assigned.

1

Hear, My Son,

About the Purposes of Proverbs

To know wisdom and instruction,

to understand words of insight.

Proverbs 1:2

WHO IS THE AUTHOR?

There are several authors of the book of Proverbs, but Solomon is generally considered the main writer. Two other authors are mentioned by name, Agur (chapter 30) and King Lemuel (chapter 31). The "wise" (men) are identified in 22:17 and 24:23 as the writers of 22:17 through 24:23.

List the name of the writers of each section of Proverbs.

Chapter 1 - 22:16 _____

Chapter 22:17 - 24:34 _____

Chapter 25:1 - 29:27 _ _____

Chapter 30 _____

Chapter 31 _____

What do 1 Kings 3:12 and 4:29-31 teach us concerning the primary author of Proverbs?

_____

_____

What evidence can you find in 1 Kings 4:32 that would connect Solomon to the writing of Proverbs?

_____

_____

TO WHOM WAS PROVERBS ADDRESSED?

It won't take you long after you begin reading Proverbs to realize that the primary person addressed and counseled is the son of the main author. Only eight verses into the first chapter you will find "my son" addressed, the first of twenty-two times. Most of the Proverbs are written primarily to Solomon's son, and secondarily to all sons.

Identify the primary and secondary addressees. Jot your name as a secondary addressee.

Primary addressee: _____

Secondary addressee: _____

WHEN WAS PROVERBS WRITTEN?

Since there are several authors and since they do not tell us when they wrote, an exact date cannot be determined. However, it is believed that all of the Proverbs may have been in existence during Solomon's lifetime (1000 B.C.), but had not been compiled into one book. Proverbs has been in existence approximately 3,000 years.

WHERE WERE THESE PROVERBS USED?

The teaching of these Proverbs was originally conducted in the palace by Solomon to his sons. He trained them in wisdom for positions in the palace. This accounts for not just the references to the home setting, but also for the many references to kings, royalty, and authority connected with life in the palace.

Look up the verses below and write the words that refer to the palace.

20:2 _____

21:1 _____

23:1-3 _____

27:23-27 _____

Other promising officials in the palace school were also taught these lessons by the sages who often addressed the students with a familiar "my son." Yet the address is also to a wider audience, that of all sons both young and old who seek after wisdom.

HOW DO WE DEFINE A PROVERB?

Dr. Bruce Waltke defines a proverb as *"a short witty saying that give use a standard by which you might judge your life."* Proverbs are probably as old as civilization itself and can be seen in the writings of almost every ancient civilization. In order for truths to be remembered they were reduced to small nuggets that could be remembered.

List a few of the proverbs used in our society today.

1. _____

2. _____

3. _____

Others quoted proverbs in the Bible. Write them.

David in 1 Samuel 24:13 _____

Samson in Judges 14:14 _____

Nathan in 2 Samuel 12:1

_____

WHY WAS PROVERBS WRITTEN?

There are many Hebrew words used in Proverbs 1:2-6 showing the purposes of the book. All of these words are synonyms for "wisdom."

Look up each verse and write the synonym next to its definition.

1. _____ (1:2a) Instructed in the truth, trained or disciplined to obey.
2. _____ (1:2b) "Common sense" helping a person see the central issue, not the surface issue.
3. _____ (1:3) Sound wisdom leading to doing what is right, just, and fair.
4. _____ (1:4) Positive shrewdness in planning one's life.
5. _____ (1:4,5) Experientially knowing the truth, having the doctrine as a part of one's life.

The first few words of Proverbs 1:2 give the primary purpose of Proverbs and 1:6 states the secondary purpose applied to proverbs in general, not just biblical proverbs.

Write the two purposes.

Primary purpose: _____

Secondary purpose: _____

FATHER-SON INTERACTION ACTIVITY 1

Identify the missing words in each verse as you note these occurrences of the phrase "my son" in Proverbs.

1:8 "Hear, my son, your _____ instruction, and forsake not your _____ teaching."

1:10 "My son, if _____ entice you, do not _____."

1:15 "My son, do not _____ in the way with them; hold back your _____ from their paths."

2:1 "My son, if you _____ my words and treasure up my _____ with you."

3:1 "My son, do not forget my teaching, but let your _____ keep my commandments."

3:11"My son, do not despise the LORD's _____ or be weary of his _____ ."

3:21 "My son, do not lose sight of _____ -- keep sound _____ and _____ ."

4:10 "Hear, my son, and accept my word, that the _____ of your life may be _____ ."

4:20 "My son, be attentive to my words; incline your _____ to my sayings."

5:1 "My son, be attentive to my wisdom; incline your _____ to my understanding."

5:20 "Why should you be _____ , my son, with a _____ woman and embrace the bosom of an adulteress?"

6:1 "My son, if you have put up _____ for your neighbor, have given your pledge to a stranger..."

6:3 "Then do this, my son, and _____ yourself, for you have come into the hand of your neighbor: go, hasten, and plead urgently with your neighbor."

6:20 "My son,_____ your father's commandment, and _____ not your mother's teaching."

7:1 "My son, _____ my words, and _____ up my commandments with you."

19:27 "_____ to hear the instruction, my son, and you will _____ from the words of knowledge."

23:15 "My son, if your _____ is wise, my heart too will be _____ ."

23:19 "_____ , my son, and be wise, and _____ your heart in the way."

23:26 "My son, give me your _____ and let your _____ observe my ways."

24:13 "My son, eat honey, for it is _____ , and the drippings of the honeycomb are sweet to your taste."

24:21 "My son, _____ the LORD and the _____ , and do not join with those who do otherwise."

27:11 "Be wise, my son, and make my heart _____ , that I may answer him who reproaches me."

FATHER-SON INTERACTION ACTIVITY 2

Look again at the "my son" verses in your Bible.

Notice the verses surrounding each occurrence and observe the various topics in the context of these verses. Don't read more than two verses before or after each verse, even though, in most cases, the context is much larger. Each topic is important because it indicates the areas where Solomon saw the need to give counsel and instruction toward being a wise and godly son.

On the following list of topics, identify the references to the verse next to the topic where it is found. Perhaps you and your father can find several other topics. Add them to the list. Note: The first ones are done for you.

TOPICS IN THE CONTEXT OF "MY SON" VERSES

GENERAL PARENTAL INSTRUCTIONS: <u>1:8; 2:1; 3:1</u>

EVIL COMPANIONS: <u>1:10; 1:15; 24:21</u>

LENGTH OF ONE'S LIFE: _____

PEACE: _____

DISCIPLINE BY GOD AND/OR PARENTS: _____

WISDOM AND DISCRETION: _____

FORBIDDEN WOMEN: _____

FINANCIAL MATTERS: _____

DISRESPECT TO PARENTS: _____

SCORNERS AND FOOLS: _____

HEART: _____

EMOTIONS OF PARENTS: _____

DRUNKENNESS: _____

GLUTTONY: _____

SLUGGARD: _____

OTHER TOPICS YOU FOUND:

1. _____
2. _____
3. _____
4. _____
5. _____

FATHER-SON INTERACTION ACTIVITY 3

Memorize Proverbs 1:5. Quiz each other on it.

COMPLETION CHECK

Check here when you complete this chapter.

FATHER _____ SON _____

Iron sharpens iron,

and one man sharpens another.

Proverbs 27:17

2

Hear, My Son,

About the Fear of the LORD

The fear of the LORD is the beginning of knowledge;

fools despise wisdom and instruction.

Proverbs 1:7

MOTTO OF THE BOOK

Many say that Proverbs 1:7 is the motto of the book of Proverbs. The words "fear of the LORD" are used repeatedly beginning in 1:7 to the last use in 24:21. Look in your Bible and count the number of times the phrase "the fear of the LORD" is used.

How many times in Proverbs is the phrase "The fear of the LORD" used? _____

This verse is the foundation for understanding the religious and theological starting point of Proverbs. Without an understanding of "the fear of the LORD," and indeed choosing the fear of the LORD (1:29), searching for wisdom is a futile endeavor. There is no consistent explanation of the world, of man, or of their workings without a knowledge of God and a fear of God. God makes sense of it all.

MEANING OF THE VERSE

"The fear of the LORD is the beginning of knowledge."

1. **"THE FEAR OF THE LORD"**

If you are to understand "the fear of the LORD" you must understand it as a response in the intellectual (mind), emotional (feeling), and volitional (will) make up of man. It is not merely an emotional (fear) response without an intellectual basis for the reaction. Nor is it just an appropriate emotional response to the content of knowledge. A genuine fear of the Lord also brings about a volitional response—an action of the will, one of obedience to the one feared, doing what He expects.

THE INTELLECTUAL RESPONSE

To have a biblical "fear of the LORD" demands that there must be an understanding of the object to be feared. The Lord Jehovah, as revealed through natural and special revelation, is exalted as the one to be feared, honored, and respected. Psalm 19 lists the natural and special revelation that reflects and contains the source of the knowledge necessary for an intellectual response.

List one word for each space that reveals these two types of revelation.

PSALM 19

Natural Revelation

- 19:1 _____

- 19.2 _____

- 19:4 _____

- 19:7 _____

- 19:8 _____

- 19:9 _____

Special Revelation

- 19:1 _____

- 19:2 _____

- 19:4 _____

- 19:7 _____

- 19:8 _____

- 19:9 _____

When we truly see God for who He is, for what He has done, and for what He can do as the Creator and Sustainer of all, when we see Him with all His many attributes, then we will reverently fear and respect Him. Proverbs 2:5 shows us that the fear of the LORD and the knowledge of God (who He is and what He is like) go hand in hand. What do you understand about God? What is He like?

List some of the attributes of God that you already know. If you have trouble filling in all the blanks, discuss God's attributes with your dad.

ATTRIBUTES OF GOD

1. _____

2. _____

3. _____

4. _____

5. _____

6. _____

7. _____

8. _____

9. _____

10. _____

THE EMOTIONAL RESPONSE

Without a physical problem, emotional responses always have some type of mental stimulus. God created man with the ability to respond emotionally. You do not just fear without a logical reason for that fear. Fear is an emotional reaction to information delivered to the mind. Therefore, if you understand who Jehovah is and what He is doing, has done, and will do, you have the necessary ingredients for developing a genuine fear of the LORD. When you see the LORD in contrast to yourself, an appropriate emotional "fear" response should occur.

Look up the verses and identify the missing word.

_____ is the response that is identifiable in Proverbs 15:33. Humility and brokenness are two responses that reveal a genuine fear of the LORD.

_____ of evil is stated in Proverbs 8:13 as an action that is equivalent to "the fear of the LORD." The person who "knows" the LORD will develop a "humility" and a "hatred for evil" along with other appropriate emotional responses as he grows in his knowledge of the LORD.

THE VOLITIONAL RESPONSE

A sincere "fear of the LORD" includes a volitional response, a choice made in the will to respond in obedience to the feared object. There is no wisdom in knowing Jehovah in all His glory and responding emotionally, yet not making the sensible choice that would identify one as wise. In fact, it is questionable whether a person genuinely knows God if he never makes decisions to obey the one he says he knows. It was he who "hated knowledge and did not to fear the LORD" in Proverbs 1:29.

2. "THE BEGINNING OF KNOWLEDGE"

"Beginning" here is significant in three ways. The "fear of the LORD" is first in order -- chronologically *first*.

The "fear of the LORD" is *first* in importance -- most important idea.

The "fear of the LORD" is *first* principle in understanding wisdom. A parallel verse in 9:10 states "The fear of the LORD is the beginning of wisdom." It is necessary to say that knowledge and wisdom are not distinguishable here. Even though there is some difference, both words are used to designate the same idea. The words are used interchangeably in the text.

Using your Bible dictionary or a regular dictionary look up these words. Define each word.

KNOWLEDGE: _____

WISDOM: _____

WISE WORDS

Dr. Bruce Waltke suggests that "wisdom" must be thought of as "a fixed, righteous order to which the wise man submits his life."

William Arnot, who wrote *Studies in Proverbs*, has said concerning "the fear of the LORD" -- "He who does not reverentially trust in God, knows nothing yet as he ought to know. His knowledge is partial and distorted. Whatever acquisitions in science he may attain, if his heart departs from the living God, he abides an ignorant man. He who in his heart says 'NO GOD' is a fool, however wise he may be in his estimation of the world, and his own."

The wise son and father make decisions every day choosing to walk and live with a deep respect and "fear of the LORD."

FATHER-SON INTERACTION ACTIVITY 1

Look up the verses, write them, and discuss them with each other.

1. What does "the fear of the LORD" mean in verses 1:7 and 9:10? What do you think the "fountain of life" represents in 14:27? _____

_____

2. What does 8:13 teach us concerning the relationship that one who fears the LORD has to evil? What else does a person who fears the LORD hate?

_____

_____

3. When are we to fear the LORD? Proverbs 23:17 How would a person do this?

_____

_____

4. What does Proverbs 15:16 tell us about that which is valuable?

_____

_____

5. Proverbs 10:27 teaches us that, "The fear of the LORD" _____
but the years of the _____ will be _____. Also read and
discuss 19:23a. How do you think this happens? Give some illustrations.

_____

_____

_____

6. List some of the benefits listed in Proverbs 22:4 of living in the fear of the LORD:

a. _____

b. _____

c. _____

Does this mean that everyone who fears the LORD will become rich? Explain.

_____

_____

How does a person grow in his fear of the LORD?

_____

_____

_____

FATHER-SON INTERACTION ACTIVITY 2

Memorize Proverbs 9:10 and quiz each other on it.

COMPLETION CHECK

Check here when you have finished chapter 2.

FATHER _____ SON _____

It has been said that

you have two ears and one mouth;

therefore, you should listen

twice as much as you speak!

3

Hear, My Son, About

Understanding Steps to Wisdom

The fear of the LORD is the beginning of wisdom,

and the knowledge of the Holy One is insight.

Proverbs 9:10

When a son has an understanding of what it means "to fear the LORD," he is then ready for his quest for wisdom. The fear of the LORD is the starting point of any intellectual pursuit. It is "the beginning of wisdom." Without an understanding of God and a fear of Him, all that is just doesn't fit together or make sense.

The LORD himself is identified as the giver of wisdom in Proverbs 2:6, "For the Lord gives wisdom." Wisdom doesn't come from a father, a teacher, or a professor. It is the goal that the father has for himself and his son. It is through his teachings that he directs his son to reach that goal. However, neither the father nor the son should be misled; without a vital relationship with God no one could possibly obtain sufficient wisdom to merit the adjective "wise."

STEP 1: WISE SONS MUST CHOOSE THE FEAR OF THE LORD

The previous chapter established that wise sons must choose the fear of the LORD. Without making this choice at the starting point of the search for wisdom, true wisdom is unattainable.

People fear various things: some fear mice, bees, spiders, snakes, elevators, water, market places or _____ *(name one of your fears)*. They fear because in their mind there is danger associated with the object of fear, a threat to their life or well-being. They make a decision to avoid or to try to kill the object of fear before it "kills" them. In other words, they make a choice *(sometimes a habit response from former choices)*, a decision of their will to take a course of action. Likewise, someone who "knows" the LORD for who He is will "fear" Him, for they realize that to ignore Him often brings life-threatening consequences. Yet one must not look only at fear as the picture of "fear and trembling" *(though it may be that for the disobedient!),* but instead it can and should be understood and practiced as a loving respect and reverence for the Lord to whom they have chosen to submit.

STEP 2: WISE SONS MUST PRAY FOR WISDOM

Proverbs 2:3 instructs the son to _____ and _____ in his pursuit of wisdom. This is perhaps the closest reference that relates to prayer in the book. To whom are sons to "cry," to pray? _____

This word "cry" is the same word used in Psalm 3:4; 28:1; 30:8; 57:2; 86:3; 120:1, and in many other verses meaning. As you pray to the Lord, who gives wisdom, you are involved in this second step necessary in your quest for wisdom.

STEP 3: WISE SONS MUST HAVE LISTENING EARS

Over and over in Proverbs we read words related to hearing times and ear times. Sons are instructed to incline and bow their ear to teaching and instruction. Both words contain the idea of **attentive, diligent listening**. But furthermore, it involves giving heed to the words and obeying them.

Review these verses and discuss.

Your ear attentive to wisdom (Proverbs 2:2): _____

Instruction and be wise (Proverbs 8:33): _____

How good are you at listening?

It has been said that you have two ears and one mouth; therefore, you should listen twice as much as you speak! (Proverbs 17:27,28). In son of the same ways we listen to a person, we listen to God. He gave us ears to listen to Him.

What are some of the times and places in which we can hear God's instruction and receive his wisdom? List your ideas and discuss them. All are opportunities to incline our ears to God and listen to Him.

1. _____   2. _____

3. _____   4. _____

5. _____   6. _____

7. _____   8. _____

How to Be a Good Listener

Listening is a way of showing a person we love and care for them, that they are worthy of our listening to them.

1. Concentrate on what the person is saying (Proverbs 1:5).

2. Let the person speak without interrupting (Proverbs 18:13).

3. Remove all distractions, if possible.

4. Take notes.

5. Ask questions (Proverbs 18:17).

6. Be sure your *body* is listening. What are some non-verbal evidences of a person who is a good listener? What does he do and not do with the parts of his body?

      Eyes: _____

      Arms: _____

      Fingers: _____

Feet: _____

Mouth: _____

Spine: _____

Discipline your body to receive the words of another (Proverbs 23:12; 24:32).

How to Be a Good Speaker

If someone is listening, another is doing the speaking. Here are guidelines for the speaker.

1. Speak carefully; guard what you say (Proverbs 21:23).

2. Be sure you know what you're talking about (Proverbs 15:2).

3. Be sure to give a wise answer to questions (Proverbs 15:28).

4. Right words at the right time bring positive results (Proverbs 15:23).

5. Know when you have said enough (Proverbs 10:19).

STEP 4: SONS MUST PUT FORTH DILIGENT EFFORT

Proverbs 2:4 tells you that you must _____ and _____ for wisdom.

The miner doesn't find silver on the outside of the mountain. Only as he diligently carves out a tunnel deep into the rock does he find the desired precious metal. Likewise, he who finds a hidden treasure doesn't find it on the surface, lest the hider be considered a fool. It takes disciplined, thought out, planned effort to find the desired objects. So it is with wisdom. If you are to find it, a deliberate, diligent, dedicated search must be made. Neither the miner nor the treasure hunter finds his bounty in one day. **To find wisdom takes time, and the longer a person perseveres the greater the prize of wisdom he will find.**

You must become a treasure hunter in the mine of wisdom. Found in the entire Bible, and not just in Proverbs, is wisdom, the diamonds of truth, those nuggets of insight that will enable you to find a meaningful relationship with the Lord and with others. It will also enable you to have success in the world in which you live.

STEP 5: WISE SONS MUST LAY CLAIM TO THE PROMISE

Read Proverbs 2:1-5. Take your pen and circle each "if" found in Proverbs 2:1,3,4. In the first four verses the "if's" present the conditions that must be met. These are the rules that must be followed, the steps that must be taken "if" wisdom is to be the reward. Circle "then" in Proverbs 2:5 and 2:9. Then you will be able to list the promises of following the steps in a successful pursuit of wisdom.

The promises are:

5-8 Knowledge and _____of God.

9-11 _____in understanding and wisdom.

12-15 Wisdom for deliverance from _____.

16-19 Wisdom for deliverance from _____.

20-22 Various benefits from _____.

FATHER-SON INTERACTION ACTIVITY 1

Together take this quiz and calculate your scores. 100 possible points.

The Father-Son Listening Quiz

1. What was the topic of the Sunday sermon? (5 pts. each) FATHER____ SON____

2. What was the topic of your last Sunday school class? (5 pts. each) FATHER____ SON____

3. What was the topic of the most recent chapel message, radio, TV, audio message, or Christian book? (5 pts. each) FATHER___ SON___

4. Give the main point of any Bible study or other service you attended (i.e., youth group, small group Bible study). (5 pts. each) FATHER___ SON___

5. How many minutes does the average American dad spend talking with his child in a week? The answer is found in the Introduction. (5 pts. each right answer) FATHER___ SON___

6. List ten of the topics in Proverbs listed around the "my son" verses. (See Chapter 1) (1 pt. for each right answer) FATHER ___ SON ___

7. Of what is the fear of the LORD the beginning? (5 pts. each) FATHER___ SON___

8. List the things from Proverbs 8:13 that a person who fears the LORD hates. (5 potential—5 pts. each) FATHER___ SON___

9. What are three responses necessary for a genuine fear of the LORD? (Chapter 2) (5 pts. each)

10. Listening is more than just hearing the words, but also includes obey them in daily action. Have you applied any knowledge you learned this week? (10 pts. for each "yes")

FATHER: YES or NO   SON: YES or NO

Total Combined Score: _____

FATHER-SON INTERACTION ACTIVITY 2

Memorize Proverbs 5:1. Quiz each other on it.

COMPLETION CHECK

Check here when you've completed Chapter 3.

FATHER _____ SON _____

4

Hear, My Son,

About Evil Companions

"My son, if sinners entice you, do not consent." Proverbs 1:10

Throughout the Old Testament we find examples in the historical books, the poetical books, and the prophets of a topic that continues strong in the New Testament. The topic of **evil companions** is found as one of the main areas of instruction, counsel, and warning. It is the first major topic upon which the father instructs his son at length. In Proverbs 1:8 the father instructs his son to "hear." In the previous chapter, we discovered in Step 3 that "hear" means: _____.

It is the father's desire at this point that his son would "hear" (obey) him concerning how to deal with "evil companions." The father's will for his son is that he would listen to "him" and not to the enticing words of these "sinners."

SON, UNDERSTAND WHO THE SINNERS ARE

In those times and throughout much of Scripture there were bands of highway robbers. The original word for "sinners" indicates that these were wicked, vicious, extremely evil men to whom sin, gross sin, had become natural habits with little conscience or concern for their victims.

SON, UNDERSTAND THE SINNER'S ENTICEMENT

Look up the meaning of the word "entice" in the dictionary and write it.

_____

The word "entice" comes from the same root word meaning "the simple." Perhaps the simple-minded, the uninstructed, the unwise young man could be persuaded or fooled into buying their offer. However, the wise son would say "NO WAY!" These "sinners" were so calloused that they were convinced within themselves that their way of life was the way to live. They were successful in enlisting many. You may say, "I could never be involved in this. This doesn't apply to me." Don't be too sure until you take a closer look at the various enticements!

THE ENTICEMENT OR LURES OF TODAY

What would be the sort of lure that a sinner could use to draw you to his cause, to become one of his group? *Identify and jot down the enticement in the blanks.*

1. THE LURE OF: _____ (1:11,12,16)

These sinners would describe their activities in the most **exciting** of terms.

- Shedding of blood

- Taking advantage of the innocent

- Killing their victims

- Putting their dead victims in graves

- Putting others into pits alive (cf. Gen. 37:20ff)

Today's sequel to this can be seen online and in every newspaper, news magazine, or TV news report. This mentality can be seen regularly in movies and many television programs.

The Get Rich Quick Lie

Television, radio, advertisements, and the daily barrage of circulars in the mail are enticements. Many of these create a desire to have some things that are "wants," not needs, things that only become wants after reading the enticing words. Credit card companies entice parents to get "one more" credit card so they can get what they want and not have to pay until later.

Murder, even mass murder, "for excitement" can be seen in our society today. So can related killings, serial murders, abuse of all types touching epidemic proportions. On a regular basis advantage is taken of innocent people. A well-known quote that describes this is: **"Come to Where the Action Is."**

2. THE LURE OF: _____ (1:13,14,19)

Money has always been a lure to the discontented in this world. *"If only I could have that 'thing.' If only I could make more money, then I would be happy and satisfied."* What does 1 Timothy 6:10 teach? *Read it together and discuss.*

The "sinner" would entice the son by promises of:

- All precious substances - all valuable things (1:13).

- Houses filled with what was stolen (1:13).

- A common lot, equal share of the money (1:14).

- A good return for the effort (1:19).

Love of the world and the things that are in the world (1 John 2:15), is the same lure in different words. This enticement has motivated many to cast a common lot with the "sinners." Today we might call the equivalent of this thievery, robbery, gambling, playing the lottery, tax evasion, cheating your employer of time, misuse of credit cards, and on and on. It is nothing more than the mentality that lures people today.

3. THE LURE OF _____ (1:14)

A desire for **companionship** and being accepted by the crowd (peer pressure) is one of the greatest lures for some teens. The lure of peer companionship was a powerful motivator in Bible days just as it is in our world today. Too often a son will reject the relationship he has with his parents to embrace a relationship with foolish friends, only to find that the latter ends in heartache both for the son and for his parents.

New Testament instructions are found in 2 Corinthians 15:33 and 2 Corinthians 6:14. *Read them and discuss.*

You can see that Paul's instruction and counsel to the believers at Corinth was similar to the father's instructions to the son. Today's motto's for the lure of companionship might be recognized by the idea of **"Be one of the crowd."**

Many advertisements try to use this lure to sell their products. *List a few.*

1. _____

2. _____

3. _____

SON, UNDERSTAND THE NECESSARY RESPONSE

The father's response is clear. He doesn't mince words with his son. They can hardly be misunderstood in these three statements:

1. *"Do not consent"* 1:10: Just say "NO!"

2. *"Do not walk in the way with them"* 1:15: Don't go with them.

3. *"Hold back your foot"* 1:15: Control yourself and stay away.

The son is to stay clear of these sinners. But the father doesn't just stop there. He gives the reason for the response.

SON, UNDERSTAND THE REASONS FOR THE RESPONSE

The reasons given are twofold:

1. It's wrong, just plain wrong. It's only for the "fools." (1:15-16)

2. They become victims of their own evil ways. "They reap what they sow." (1:18)

SON, UNDERSTAND THE TWO POSSIBLE MEANINGS OF PROVERBS

"For in vain is a net spread in the sight of any bird." (1:17)

This verse must be understood by identifying who the bird is in the proverb. It could represent the "sinner" or the son who has already been instructed and warned.

1. If it represents the "sinner" it means that in his desire for excitement, money, companionship, and this way of life, he will proceed even though a net to trap him is in plain view. He has seen others get trapped, yet somehow he thinks he is not going to get caught.

2. If the bird represents the "son" who has been instructed by his father, the proverb means that to see the net (the end of the sinners reaping what they have sown) is all the son needs to be able to say "NO!" to the sinner's appeal. A wise son who sees the trap will never get caught in it.

FATHER-SON INTERACTION ACTIVITY 1

List the characteristics of evil companions found in these verses. Evaluate two friends.

FRIEND 1: _____ FRIEND 2: _____

2:12 _____

2:14, 4:16 _____

4:17 _____

6:13 _____

6:14 _____

12:10, 12:13, 12:21 _____

14:17, 15:28 _____

17:11 _____

17:23 _____

20:19 _____

21:10 _____

24:2 _____

28:1 _____

28:4 _____

FATHER-SON INTERACTION ACTIVITY 2

Look through magazines or online articles for examples of types of enticements of the "sinners" (Excitement, Money, and Companionship). Find examples of all three. Discuss what you find.

FATHER-SON INTERACTION ACTIVITY 3

Memorize Proverbs 1:10. Quiz each other on it.

COMPLETION CHECK

Check here when you've completed Chapter 4.

FATHER _____ SON _____

5

Hear, My Son, About

Developing Quality Friendships

Iron sharpens iron, and one man sharpens another.

Proverbs 27:17

Everyone needs friends! Just as the father counseled his son about avoiding evil companions, he also counseled his son about how to develop quality friendships -- by interacting properly with one another. He warned his son against destroying good friendships by inappropriate actions or attitudes. Then he wisely instructed his son on the qualities that build true and lasting friendships.

The translators of Proverbs recognized different levels of friendship. Generally the same word used in the Hebrew language was translated as "friend" or as "neighbor," depending upon the context or upon the particular meaning of the Proverb. **Usually "friend" was used to identify a close or intimate relationship**, whereas "neighbor" was used to identify a casual relationship or acquaintance.

For example, in Proverbs 26:18,19 the word was translated "neighbor" because a bad practical joke is inappropriate to close and intimate friendships. In Proverbs 17:17 the word was translated "friend" because casual acquaintances don't love at all times. In some verses, the word could be translated interchangeably without altering the meaning.

In his book about special friendships, Guy Greenfield observed eight levels of relationships: avoidance, greeting, separate-interests, common interests, social interaction, caring, sharing, and intimacy. As the relationship level deepens, the number of people with whom we relate grows smaller. For example, we may say hello to hundreds, share in a common interest group with thirty, care about twelve, share with only five or six, and be intimate with three, two, one, or none. **The deeper the level of friendship, the more time is required to nurture it**. Thus, Proverbs 18:24 tells us that the man who has many friends must take the time to show himself as a friend. But he may have only "a friend" that sticks closer than a brother, an intimate friend with whom he can develop a "Jonathan-David" relationship (1 Samuel 20:17).

The father in Proverbs desired to help his son avoid the pitfalls that destroy friendships. Though it takes time and effort to develop good friendships, it seems all too easy to destroy them. Proverbs 18:19 declares that once we have wounded a close friendship, it is very difficult to restore. The wise son will learn to build, not destroy, as he develops deeper levels of friendships that are pleasant to both and will "sharpen each other" (27:17).

AVOID THESE CHARACTERISTICS THAT DESTROY FRIENDSHIPS

There are many actions and attitudes that hinder relationships with others. The wise son will take note of these and examine his own friendships. *Identify the missing words.*

Seeking friendships because of _____ (19:6).

Proverbs 19:6a says, "Many seek the favor of a generous man." The man was an influential person, causing many to desire his "friendship" for the gain that it brought to themselves. The man was being warned that some would desire his friendship only for what they could get. Perhaps they just enjoyed "dropping names" to build up themselves in the eyes of others. Usually a friendship based on the **influence** of the other brought expectations or special favors. To have an influential friend seems to make a person feel important in some way. Yet how empty that relationship must feel, both to the person being used and to the one who takes advantage of the other!

Seeking friendships for _____ (19:6b).

Proverbs 19:6b continues, "Every man is a friend to him that gives gifts." Proverbs 14:20 warned, "...the rich has many friends." These verses imply that **personal gain** is a wrong motive behind true friendship. Again we see a desire to "get" rather than to give. To be taken advantage of because of wealth destroys true friendship.

Seeking friendships by using _____ (29:5).

Proverbs 29:5 says that the man who flatters his neighbor is spreading a net in which either one or both may be caught. **Flattery** will not enhance a friendship! The man who flatters will eventually be caught by his own words of deceit. His dishonesty builds a trap that destroys the possibility of a true friendship developing. The wise son will be alert to the trap of another's flattery and will avoid building a friendship upon this dishonest foundation.

Other characteristics that destroy friendships

The father gave his son several other Proverbs that warned him against characteristics that would destroy his friendships. A wise son will examine himself to be sure these characteristics are not found in his own life.

Look up these verses and list the inappropriate actions that destroy friendship.

NEGATIVE ACTION

3:29 _____

17:9 _____

21:10 _____

22:24 _____

25:9,10 _____

25:20 _____

26:18,19 _____

27:6b _____

27:14 _____

BUILD THESE CHARACTERISTICS THAT DEVELOP FRIENDSHIPS

The father recognized that his son must not only avoid negative character traits, but that he must **build positive qualities into his friendships**. Solomon must have heard stories of his father's intimate friend, Jonathan, who saved David's life even at the risk of his own (1 Samuel 19:1-20:42). Jonathan and David had a love and friendship (1 Samuel 18:3,4) that surely served as a role model for Solomon, and then for some of his sons. Theirs was a **wholesome**, intimate friendship between two men that was mutually beneficial.

A true friend _____ (27:10).

A friend, or even an older friend of the family, was not to be neglected by the sons, because a friend nearby would be more available to **help in times of trouble** than a brother who lived far away. Mutual help is implied as two families lived near each other and often helped each other. Quite naturally their mutual friendship would grow, perhaps finally reaching the ideal of friends sticking closer than brothers (18:24). This type of friend should be cherished. In fact, it is sin not to love him (14:21).

A true friend _____ (17:17).

The friend in this verse is probably in contrast with the brother in the second part. This would mean that the friend **loves at all times** and is born for adversity as well, and that the brother loves at all times and is born for adversity. Both are equal sources of strength and encouragement in times of trouble. The true friend and the brother will both love and be willing to help at all times, whatever the circumstances, in good times and in hard times. The wise son not only desires to have this kind of friend, but is also willing to be this kind of friend.

A true friend _____ (27:9).

It seems that everyone will give counsel, but not everyone **gives wise, godly counsel.** This man's friend did just that, and it led to a sweet or pleasant result. Hearty counsel is paralleled in this passage to "perfume and ointment," with "joy and rejoicing in one's heart" resulting from the counsel.

Some sons fail to use their parents as a primary source of wise counsel. Most parents stand ready to counsel their children into wise decisions. Parental counsel is often handed down from other godly people to the parents. **Parents often learn from trial and error in their own lives.** These experiences over many years make them better prepared to give good advice than a son's peers. Sons may find that the counsel of their peers agrees more with their own desires, yet may lead to heartache and more problems. A wise son won't get caught following the poor counsel of peers as Rehoboam did after rejecting the wise counsel of the older men. (1 Kings 12:1-17).

A true friend _____ (17:9).

To "cover over" means to be silent about a matter rather than to repeat it. When one **covers a transgression** he is silent about an offense and is practicing forgiveness. He that is not silent separates close friendships. To practice forgiveness means to keep silent in three areas:

1. He will be silent to the offending party by not bringing up the offense to him again.

2. He will be silent to others, not repeating the offense to others not involved.

3. He will keep silent to himself, not reviewing the offense in his own mind.

To apply these principles promotes love between the two parties involved in an offense. Love "covers" all sins (10:12). It is to a man's glory to forgive rather than to become angry over an offense (19:11).

A true friend _____ (27:6).

The ability to take personal criticism that causes pain depends to a large degree upon the relationship one has with the criticizer. A faithful friend **tells you your fault** because he is committed to you and desires to help rather than hurt you. He is just like a parent whose discipline inflicts hurt for a time but ultimately reaps positive results (20:30; 19:18). The Hebrew word describes this friend as one who "loves," one who is motivated to help his intimate friend to strengthen his character. His openness and honesty which may cause a wound for now is intended to produce positive rather than negative responses. In a healthy, growing friendship, each friend "sharpens" the countenance of the other by strengthening the inner character and emotions that shine out through the face, even as iron smooth out rough spots in another piece of iron (27:17). Proverbs 28:23 says that in the end this friend will be appreciated more than the one who flatters and says the fault is really okay.

A true friend _____ (25:17).

A friend knows when enough is enough. He knows when to come to your house, but he also **knows when to leave**. He knows when he's been there long enough. He certainly doesn't want his friend to get sick of him. *Compare verse 16 to verse 17.*

What is enough?

_____

_____

What is the result of too much?

_____

_____

A true friend _____ (6:1-5).

This young man got caught in the snare of co-signing for his friend's debt. His father gave him wise counsel to get out of the agreement. He told him that he **should never be a guarantee for another's financial debt.**

What phrases show how serious the father thought this problem really was?

a. _____

b. _____

c. _____

d. _____

e. _____

What attitude did the father tell the son he must have toward his friend? (6:3)

_____

_____

What would make sure, or "guarantee," the son's friendship? (6:5)

_____

_____

If the friend refused to let him out of the deal, what do you think would happen to the friendship?

_____

_____

What are some of the complications of the practice of co-signing when the first party cannot pay his debt?

a. _____

b. _____

c. _____

FATHER-SON INTERACTION ACTIVITY 1

First, review the negative characteristics that destroy friendships. Privately, not in a group, discuss examples from your experience or your Dad's experience where those you know have displayed these characteristics and how it affected their friendships. Be sure not to allow gossip, breaking confidences, or spreading rumors (17:9; 25:9,10) be one of your characteristics during this assignment!

Second, review the positive qualities that build friendships. Discuss examples from your experience or your Dad's experience where those you know have displayed these qualities. Now consider this questions.

a. How did it affect their ability to make and keep friends?

_____

_____

b. How did you feel about each?

_____

_____

c. How did they feel about you?

_____

_____

d. Why is/is not each still your friend?

_____

_____

FATHER-SON INTERACTION ACTIVITY 2

Work together with your father to develop a project that would eliminate one negative quality you manifest in your friendships. It must be replaced by the positive quality related to it.

(This is the put off, put on principle from Ephesians 4:22-24 with examples in 4:25-32.)

Below is an example of a project, but you may choose any area in which you have a problem. Choose a friend to focus on as you develop the positive quality of friendship.

PUT OFF: UNCONTROLLED ANGER (PROVERBS 22:24).

PUT ON: CONTROLLED ANGER (PROVERBS 19:11).

Keep a daily log (journal) of every time you become angry. Write down how you handled the situation, and how you should have handled the situation to please the Lord. Devise a plan to report daily to your father about how you did and to seek his counsel in tough situations. Set up a system of rewards and losses.

FATHER-SON INTERACTION ACTIVITY 3

Memorize Proverbs 18:24. Quiz each other on it.

COMPLETION CHECK

Check here when you've completed Chapter 5.

FATHER _____ SON _____

Hear, my son,

your father's instruction,

and forsake not

your mother's teaching.

Proverbs 1:8

6

Hear, My Son, About

Honoring Your Parents

Hear, my son, your father's instruction,

and forsake not your mother's teaching.

Proverbs 1:8

Your parents should be your most important relationship on earth this side of marriage. **They are the primary influence upon you throughout your most impressionable years of life.** It is mainly their model as man and woman, husband and wife, father and mother that will help to mold your understanding of these important roles and relationships.

When our LORD gave Moses the Ten Commandments at Mount Sinai, He gave the parent-child commandment fifth, right after the first four commandments pertaining to man's relationship to God. Exodus 20:12 reads, "Honor your father and your mother, that your days may be long in the land that the LORD your God is giving you." In the New Testament this same command is restated in Ephesians 6:1-3.

In the book of Proverbs this command is nowhere stated. However, it is the basis and foundational thought for the father's statements. It is with a full understanding of the fifth commandment that the father instructs his son concerning the development of his relationship to his parents. All that is said reflects a broad understanding of the father's wisdom in how a son may honor his parents.

HONOR YOUR PARENTS BY HEARING THEM

We have already established in Chapter 3 that "to hear" implies much more than just listening to words with our ears. It means: _____. It is a fact that without a practice of this definition there is no possibility of "honoring your parents," because honoring means being obedient to their teachings and instructions. To honor them means to listen carefully to their counsel (1:8; 2:1; 3:1).

Several times in Proverbs, the father and mother stand together as the instructor of the children. **Even though the father is primarily recognized and responsible for the training of the child, the mother is found by his side complementing the same task.** We see this in Proverbs 1:8 and 6:20.

Jot down what a wise son hears.

A wise son will hear:

1:8 _____

1:8; 6:20 _____

6:20 _____

All three, the instruction, the law, and the commandments, were to be heard by the son. This implies that the parents who orally spoke these teachings were already full of wisdom. What they communicated was that which the son needed in order to be wise. "Hearing" produced a wise son; he who forsook wisdom was a foolish son.

    HEARING = _____

    FORSAKING = _____

HONOR YOUR PARENTS BY BEING SENSITIVE TO THEIR EMOTIONS

Just as the son has emotional wants that parents can meet, the parents have emotional wants and desires that their children can meet. The wise son will seek to meet those desires as he loves, honors, and compliments his parents (17:6; 31:28).

A foolish son brings "hurt" to his parents.

As a foolish son rejects his parents' teachings he lives a life of disobedience. He brings hurt to himself, but not to himself only. He also brings great pain to the emotional life and often the physical life of his parents.

"None of us lives to himself" (Romans 14:7), neither is any man an island. His life, whether negative or positive, affects many people. The unmarried son's first impact will be upon his parents. If he dishonors his parents by rejecting their words, the emotional result to his parents will be traumatic.

1. Hurt to his mother: In Proverbs 10:1 we are told that "a foolish son is a **sorrow** to his mother." The foolish son brings deep grief and anguish to his mother. Heaviness has the meaning of deep sorrow which tears the heart, producing great pain. Other verses that contain a description of the foolish son's emotional impact on his mother are:

EMOTIONAL RESPONSE

17:21 _____

17:25 _____

19:26 _____

2. Hurt to his father: Proverbs 17:21 tells us that the father of a fool has no joy. In Proverbs 19:13 the foolish son is described as bringing "ruin" to his father. This means that the son is no longer a blessing to the family but is looked upon as "a troublesome evil and a very great misfortune." Other verses that describe the foolish son's emotional impact of his father are:

EMOTIONAL RESPONSE

17:25 _____

28:7 _____

A wise son brings "HAPPINESS" to his parents.

1. Happiness to his mother: Two words describe the emotions that a wise son brings to his mother. These words are "joy" and "rejoicing." Rejoicing contains the idea of intense joy--joy with excitement. What a contrast to the grief and sorrow brought to the mother of the fool.

EMOTIONAL RESPONSE

23:24 _____

28:7; 23:25 _____

2. Happiness to his father

The emotional responses of the father are ones of **gladness and rejoicing**. "Glad" and "rejoice" are each found several times to describe the father's emotional response to his son's wise decisions of life.

EMOTIONAL RESPONSE

10:1 _____

15:20 _____

23:24 _____

23:25 _____

29:3 _____

Children need to visualize the emotional impact of their actions upon their parents. Perhaps it would change the outcome of their lives if they were motivated to "honor their parents."

HONOR YOUR PARENTS BY AVOIDING THE CONSEQUENCES OF THE FOOL

The fool is described in Proverbs 11:29 as one that "troubles his own household." The word "troubles" means: _____.

By his own foolish actions, this son distresses his entire house. All those who live in that house are touched by it. The reward for doing so is to inherit the wind. He ends up with nothing. This is the empty reward of the foolish son. Some other verses that list the consequences of the fool are:

EMOTIONAL RESPONSE

15:10 _____

19:13 _____

20:20 _____

30:17 _____

Proverbs 20:20 says that the son who dishonors his parents will have "his lamp will be put out in utter darkness." William Wilson, in his book *Old Testament Word Studies,* said this about the lamp:

> Lamps in the East were kept burning all night. The origin of the custom may have been to preserve themselves from the serpents and other noxious reptiles; hence, the putting out of a light is a figure of great danger as the light is a symbol of prosperity.

> The fool who mocks his father and despises his mother brings great danger to his life and his prosperity. These are some of the consequences to those who dishonor their parents and choose to reject wisdom.

HONOR YOUR PARENTS BY STRIVING FOR THE REWARDS OF THE WISE

The rewards of the wise are found throughout the book of Proverbs and especially in the many verses contrasting the wise and the foolish. However, Proverbs 1:9 mentions two rewards that show the person who receives them as truly wise and in a position to receive other rewards. "Hearing," obeying and honoring your parents will bring the rewards of:

1. _____   2._____

It is hard to tell whether these rewards are literal, figurative, or both. Beautiful adornments to the head and neck were given to wise sons, indicating to others that they had embraced the teachings and instructions of their parents which resulted in wise living.

FATHER-SON INTERACTION ACTIVITY 1

1. *Evaluate whether you are bringing any emotional "hurt" to your parents in any way* (Prov. 17:21).

Are they pleased or displeased and why?

_____

What areas of behavior do you need to change in order to bring pleasure to your parents?

_____

After you think through this, ask your father to add insights in these areas.

2. *Ask each parent individually and privately if you are hurting either of them in any way.*

Ask their forgiveness for any hurts, past or present.

3. *Ask your father to help you recognize in the future the times you bring hurt to either parent so that you can correct wrong responses or habit patterns.*

4. *Sit down separately with your mother and father and their individual "Love List," below.*

Discuss with each of them the ways you could improve your expressions of love to each of them. Then highlight the numbers you are neglecting. Ask them to add others things you did not highlight. Choose several items on each list and purpose this week to show love to your parents.

75 Ways You Can Show Love to your Mother

1. Make dinner for her (or help with dinner or set the table).

2. Buy or pick flowers for her.

3. Clean your room without being asked.

4. Do dishes without being asked.

5. Write her notes or send her cards.

6. Talk to her.

7. Give her a hug and tell her you love her.

8. Help with housework.

9. Spend time with her.

10. Have a good attitude.

11. Always be kind.

12. Speak in a nice way (don't back talk).

13. Help her when she's sick.

14. Help with the wash or fold clothes.

15. Learn to iron your own things.

16. Don't fight with your brothers and sisters.

17. Respect her and obey her.

18. Clean up your own messes.

19. Pass all your courses in school.

20. Help with pets.

21. Give her gifts (Christmas, Birthday, and Mother's Day).

22. Cheer her up when she has a bad day.

23. Pray for her. Pray with her.

24. Tell her the truth.

25. Stay out of trouble.

26. Stay out of her things; respect her privacy.

27. Bake a cake for her.

28. Give her a box of candy.

29. Give her breakfast in bed.

30. Take more responsibility.

31. Take out the trash.

32. Rake the leaves and do yard work for her.

33. Throw a birthday party for her.

34. Run errands for her.

35. Go to church with her.

36. Take care of your younger brothers and sisters to help her out.

37. Wash and wax her car.

38. Remember her birthday and Mother's Day.

39. Listen to her when she's had a hard day.

40. Have devotions with her.

41. Give your mom and dad some time together.

42. Take her out for lunch.

43. Learn from her. Listen to her advice.

44. Say "thank you" for the things she does for you.

45. Kiss her goodnight.

46. Go shopping with her and help her.

47. Memorize verses.

48. Make lunch some Saturdays or prepare Sunday breakfast.

49. Babysit willingly for your younger siblings.

50. Behave in school and stay out of trouble.

51. Make coffee for her in the morning.

52. Open the door for her.

53. Don't complain about what's for supper.

54. Hang up your clothes.

55. Pump gas for her.

56. Joke around with her.

57. Be glad to see her when you come home.

58. Take her out to eat at a nice restaurant.

59. Make her feel like she's wanted.

60. Get up in the morning when she calls.

61. Praise her when talking with friends.

62. Don't argue with her.

63. Let her choose the TV program.

64. Live for God.

65. Write or call often when you are away from home.

66. Stay home with her sometimes instead of going out with friends.

67. Respect the standards she's set for you.

68. Thank her for the way she has brought you up.

69. Help get the younger kids ready in the morning.

70. Get home at the agreed upon time.

71. Mind your manners.

72. Don't beg for things all the time.

73. Accept the fact you can't have everything you want or do everything you ask.

74. Just be there when she needs someone.

75. Help her out financially sometimes.

75 Ways You Can Show Love to Your Father

1. Do your chores with a right attitude.

2. Obey him.

3. Help him when he builds things or with whatever he is doing.

4. Give him little gifts that are meaningful to him.

5. Get good grades/study harder.

6. Listen to his advice and correction.

7. Tell him "I love you."

8. Don't talk back or be disrespectful.

9. Pray for him. Pray with him.

10. Thank him for what he does and what he provides.

11. Say goodbye before you leave for school in the morning.

12. Play football/basketball with him.

13. Don't fight with brothers and sisters.

14. Don't ask for a lot of unnecessary money.

15. Go places with him.

16. Clean your room without being told.

17. Make him coffee and breakfast.

18. Buy him candy (unless, of course, he's diabetic!).

19. Give him a hug.

20. Give the dog a bath.

21. Care for him when he's sick.

22. Develop a habit for personal devotions.

23. Run to the store for him or do other errands.

24. Start the car to get it warmed up.

25. Write him a note or send him a card.

26. Help him carry things into the house.

27. Rub his back.

28. Help with the outside work.

29. Kiss him.

30. Buy him presents (Birthday, Christmas, Father's Day, etc.).

31. Have a good attitude in general.

32. Be responsible.

33. Wash and clean the car or truck.

34. Dish up ice cream or make dessert for him.

35. Tell him you love him and cheer him up when he's not having a good day.

36. Be what he wants you to be within the confines of godly character.

37. Have a good attitude toward him.

38. Take him out to dinner.

39. Say "hello" when he comes home.

40. Take him to a football game.

41. Give him money when he needs it.

42. Help him with his work if he works at home.

43. Get interested in his hobbies.

44. Have devotions with him and your mom.

45. Leave your mom and him alone for their times together.

46. Plan an outing for the family.

47. Be kind to him.

48. Respect him.

49. Clean the house when mom's not home.

50. Let him watch what he wants on TV.

51. Get the paper for him.

52. Throw a birthday party for him.

53. Help him relax after work.

54. Polish his shoes.

55. Stay out of his things; respect his privacy.

56. Thank him for what he gets for you.

57. Spend time with him.

58. Love your mom.

59. Be patient.

60. Be a good example and try not to embarrass him.

61. Be ready to go somewhere when he says it's time to leave.

62. Let him help you with homework.

63. Babysit so he can take your mother out to dinner.

64. Give him time to settle in when he gets home from work.

65. Don't slam the door when he's taking a nap.

66. Don't throw away his beat up old clothes until he's ready.

67. Act like his jokes are funny; listen to his "olden days" stories.

68. Don't go near his tool chest without permission.

69. Get the mail and leave it in the designated place.

70. Tell him you are thankful God gave him to you.

71. Be as good an athlete as you can be.

72. Thank him for the way he brought you up.

73. Help your mother when he's not around.

74. Tell him he's the best dad in the whole world.

75. Don't ignore him when he talks.

FATHER-SON INTERACTION ACTIVITY 2

Ask your dad to help you identify foolish activities or attitudes in your life. Together find Scriptures that deal with the root problem. Ask him for counsel on how to become wise in that area of life.

FATHER-SON INTERACTION ACTIVITY 3

Memorize Proverbs 10:1. Quiz each other on it.

COMPLETION CHECK

Check here when you've completed Chapter 6.

FATHER _____ SON _____

7

Hear, My Son, About Discipline

My son, do not despise the LORD's discipline or be weary of his reproof,

for the LORD reproves him who he loves, as a father the son in whom he delights.

Proverbs 3:11-12

From the beginning of time, man was created with the ability to make choices. He was not made as a robot, programmed to perform the desires and will of his Creator. Man was made with a will to choose. That means that he can decide whom he will love and obey and also whom he will not love or obey, as well as which instructions he will receive and which instructions he will reject. Man's will is his to control.

This truth down through the centuries has brought with it blessings and curses. Adam and Eve chose to disobey, bringing sin and its curses upon mankind. Christ chose to obey, bringing the opportunity of blessing unto eternal life to all who would believe.

To obey or to disobey is the choice each son has as he exercises his will. His obedient response to God's instruction and discipline, and to that of his parents as well, is not something that can be programmed, predicted, or pressured into conformity. Every individual has to decide for himself what his response will be.

Proverbs 22:6 reads, "Train up a child in the way he should go; even when he is old he will not depart from it."

Some godly parents who have done everything humanly possible to "train up" their children have had one or more of their children rebel, disobey the parents' instructions, and live the life of a fool. In contrast, there have been some ungodly parents who have had no concept of "training-up" their children, yet, their sons have matured, have become wise, and have been used of God to bring blessing to many. Each son chose to exercise his will against the training given by the parents.

"Train Up a Child" Truth

Sons need to know that many parents have struggled emotionally under guilt from this verse in Proverbs. This verse is not a promise but a general principle. Those parents saw the verse as a promise and attempted to train up their children in the right paths only to find some of them departing from that path later in life.

PROVERBS 22:6, Not a _____

Sons need to know that many parents have struggled emotionally under guilt from this verse in Proverbs. This verse is **not a promise** but a general principle. Those parents saw the verse as a promise and attempted to train up their children in the right paths only to find some of them departing from that path later in life. They know God's Word is true. Therefore, they concluded that they had failed in some way. They must have done something wrong. They hang their heads in embarrassment and shame looking for the mistakes. However, these parents might have done very little wrong. They may have been model parents whose son chose to reject his parents' instructions and chose to follow the wrong path.

Some sons have blamed their parents for lack of training and have used their parents' legitimate failure as an excuse to live for the world. They reason that if their parents had done a better job they would have turned out properly.

However, the truth in both situations above is that **sons have a choice**. They can choose against the godly model and training of their parents and rebel, while others can choose against the ungodly training and model of their parents and obey.

***PROVERBS 22:6, But a** _____*

This verse must be seen as **a general principle** and not as a promise. It is generally true. As Solomon looked upon life around him, he concluded that this is what generally happens when godly parents train up their children. But it is not a promise, or the outcome could always be guaranteed in spite of the will of the child. Parent modeling and training are important. Children generally are a product of their parents. However, they are not robots that will all "turn out" wise at the end of the assembly line if everything right is programed into them along the way. Parent training must be a major factor in the son's upbringing which will have its effect. Generally, children with godly parent-models and godly training will be godly when they are old. Yet **we are not to conclude that if a son turns out to be a fool the parents have failed**. It may indicate that, but the son still had the choices to make.

The conclusion of this matter is, "Sons, it is really up to you." If parents train you well, you still can obey or disobey. If your parents give you no training or even ungodly training, you can still obey or disobey. The choice is yours because God gave you the freedom to decide for yourself. It is God's will as well as your parents' desire that you choose wisdom.

DISCIPLINE IS PART OF THE "TRAINING UP" OF A SON

There are two ingredients necessary in the disciplining of sons. Both are necessary if the parents are going to carry out their responsibility in a God directed manner.

Ingredient 1: Instruction

This word involves the father attempting to reach the mind of the son through words to show wisdom as the desired behavior. "Hearing" is what the father desires as he instructs the son.

Just for review, what does hearing involve? _____ (Chapter 3)

Ingredient 2: Chastise; Rebuke; Reproof

All three words involve not only words of training but primarily the actions of discipline. This is the action part of training where the father attempts to reach the senses or the "seat" of the son, trying through action, or structured training, not necessarily through words. It is obvious in Proverbs that instruction leading to wisdom is stressed. The father desires to teach the son about the way in which he should go. He shows him and instructs him in the path that leads to happiness. The father also realizes that "folly is bound of in the heart of a child, but the rod of discipline drives it far from him" (22:15). The wise father knows that there is a time to stop verbal instruction and move to a structured program of reward and loss.

DISCIPLINE IS AN ACTION OF LOVE

What a strange, almost paradoxical, statement! On the surface most sons will not be able to see the truth in it. However, when a father disciplines a son God's way, he is showing his son how much he really **loves** him.

In fact, when God disciplines his children he gives us the example to follow in method and motivation. Proverbs 3:11-12 and 13:24 tell us that the motivation behind God's discipline and a father's discipline is that of _____.

The son is warned not to mistake about what is really happening. He is not to become weary, neither to despise nor to resent the discipline of God nor of his father, because both are signs of love rather than hatred (13:24).

DISCIPLINE IS AN ACTION OF HOPE

If your father ceases to discipline you, it shows you the hopelessness he feels in the continuing of your training. Discipline shows that the father has **hope** that a foolish action or attitude in his son can still be eliminated and a wise one disciplined to replace it.

If your father has ceased to discipline you, it can be for two reasons. Either he has seen the desired positive change, or he has become hopeless that any change will ever occur. Discipline is also motivated by _____.

DISCIPLINE REJECTED IS AN ACT OF STUPIDITY

The word "brutish" in the original language also means "stupid" (12:1). In this verse the son who rejects correction is stupid. None likes the idea of being called stupid. But that is exactly what God calls the son who rejects discipline!

Look up the verses and find further description of the person who rejects discipline and instruction. Jot down the description.

DESCRIPTION

13:1 _____

15:5 _____

12:1 _____

13:18 _____

15:32 _____

19:27 _____

22:15 _____

29:15 _____

DISCIPLINE RECEIVED IS AN ACTION OF WISDOM

Proverbs 29:15 states that "the rod and reproof give wisdom." When your father reproves you and/or uses the rod on you and you receive it properly, it is an action of wisdom for both you and your father. For your father it is wise because he recognizes both his responsibility and the benefits to his son. For you it is wise because when discipline is received with the right attitude it "yields the peaceful fruit of righteousness" (Hebrews 12:11).

Look up the verses and list the description of receiving discipline in a godly way.

DESCRIPTION

12:1 _____

13:1 _____

13:18 _____

15:5 _____

15:31 _____

20:30 _____

23:13-14 _____

29:15 _____

29:17 _____

FATHER-SON INTERACTION ACTIVITY 1

Ask your father if there are any areas in which he has stopped disciplining you and what his reasons were for stopping. Ask him to give you another chance if there's hope for change. Rejoice with him in the areas of positive change already accomplished, and keep up the good work!

FATHER-SON INTERACTION ACTIVITY 2

Thank your father for the time he spends in your training and the love he shows you by disciplining you. Thank him especially for the times he has spent with you in working on these lessons.

FATHER-SON INTERACTION ACTIVITY 3

With your father discuss four or five weak areas in your training. Set up a plan to turn these weak areas into strengths. Work together on it with your father, becoming accountable to him primarily. Let your mother know what areas you are working on so that she can act as "back-up" for your father when he is not at home. With your father, list an effective reward and loss for each of the desired areas of change.

Father-Helping-Son Change Project

CHANGE DESIRED / REWARD / LOSS

1.

2.

3.

4.

5.

Initialed by FATHER _____ SON _____

FATHER-SON INTERACTION ACTIVITY 4

Memorize Proverbs 3:11,12. Quiz each other on it.

COMPLETION CHECK

Check here when you've completed Chapter 7.

FATHER _____ SON _____

Too little sleep or too much sleep

bring harmful effects on the body

which have their own consequences.

8

Hear, My Son, About

Working and Laziness

Go to the ant, O sluggard; consider her ways, and be wise.

Proverbs 6:6

Many people look at work as a necessary evil. They see it as a part of God's curse on Adam after the fall of man. Some envision that if sin had never come mankind would live in a state of eternal bliss, no one needing to work. They envision a world of personal "good times" centered on a continual fellowship with God.

With that concept no wonder so many people resent having to work and to earn a living! However, that idea contradicts the truth of God's Word concerning work. That view more clearly describes the thinking of the sluggard who wants and desires many things, but who doesn't have the motivation to work to acquire them.

God's design in creation was that man would work. It was part of man's activity before the Fall. Genesis 2:15 teaches us that when God put man in the Garden of Eden, his job was to work it and take care of it. "Sweat" and "painful toil" seem to be the only addition to the work after sin. In Proverbs the wise son is one who is diligent in his work and is therefore rewarded appropriately for a job well done. In contrast to the diligent worker is the sluggard. His goal concerning work is to do as little as possible and still get by. This eventually catches up to him and the natural consequences of this attitude take over.

A WISE SON HAS WISE WORK HABITS

Solomon taught his son to have wise work habits. He showed him several important work principles that were observable in nature. He had his son observe an ant colony and brought to his son's attention the ants' wise work habits. If the son learned from the ants, he was wise (Proverbs 6:6-11).

Look up the references and fill in the blanks.

1. The Wise Son Will _____ (6:7)

In Proverbs 6:7, the ant is described as an insect who works well without a "guide, overseer, or ruler." The ant has no boss, yet it works the same as if a boss were looking over its shoulder. It is rare today to find someone who will work like the ant and put as much industry into his job when his boss is absent. When a son is found having the quality of diligence, that son will soon be a boss (12:24). He shall have authority over many others.

2. The Wise Son Will _____ (6:8)

In Proverbs 6:8 we learn that in the summer the ant gathers and provides enough food for the colony for the winter season. The wise son will work when it is available so that he can provide for the needs of himself and his household. Today's welfare mentality is opposite to the lesson taught by the ant. **An able-bodied person is to work and provide for his own**. God expects that of His creation. This principle heartily supports the idea of 2 Thessalonians 3:10. The natural consequence of not working is not eating.

3. The Wise Son Will _____ (6:8)

In Proverbs 6:8 we learn another lesson from the ant. In summer and harvest, when the weather was good, he would do his work. The ant didn't schedule work in the winter because the cold and perhaps snow would prevent him from gathering and providing what he needed. If he didn't work at the set times he paid the consequences later.

4. The Wise Son _____ (6:9)

In Proverbs 6:9, the questions to the sluggard of "how long" and "when" will you sleep implies that the wise son should have a sleep schedule. Every person needs a certain amount of sleep. Too little sleep or too much sleep bring harmful effects on the body which have their own consequences. In this case the wise son will schedule his day so that he can receive adequate rest to be most productive in whatever he does.

THE SLUGGARD HAS UNWISE WORK HABITS

In many of the passages that describe the sluggard, the father's humor is seen as he describes a sluggard to his son. In looking at the sluggard's habits the father desires that his son would see and develop the opposite quality.

Look up the references, and fill in the blanks.

1. The Sluggard _____ (6:9,10)

Proverbs 20:13 describes the sluggard as one who loves sleep. The humor can be seen when Solomon says he doesn't just lie in his bed, but is hinged to it like a door in a doorway that swings back and forth (26:14).

2. The Sluggard _____ (10:4)

Work—A Necessary Evil?

Many people look at work as a necessary evil. They see it as a part of God's curse on Adam after the Fall of man. Some envision that if sin had never come mankind would live in a state of eternal bliss, no one needing to work. They envision a world of personal "good times" centered on a continual fellowship with God.

With that concept no wonder so many people resent having to work and to earn a living!

Proverbs 10:4 says he works with a "slack" hand. The word here seem to combine the words slothful and deceitful. This poor person has come to poverty because he has deceived his employer and broken his trust by pretending to work when in reality he was doing nothing.

3. The Sluggard _____ (22:13, 26:13)

The humor is again seen in this principle as the sluggard uses the excuse that his life would be in danger if he went to work. He reported that there was a loose lion in the streets (22:13; 26:13).

The excuse may be humorous, yet the excuses that many give today for missing work or missing church are even more humorous!

4. The Sluggard _____ (13:4)

The sluggard has desires for many things. **His inactivity gives him much time to think, covet, and desire to have**, yet the motivation to get up and work is not part of his character. The humor is seen again when his hands (as if hands could think for themselves) refuse to do any work (21:25-26). He would like the pay to purchase that which he desires, but he will not force his hands to cooperate!

5. The Sluggard _____ (24:30,31)

The sluggard is not only just a poor employee but if he should have his own business it is certain to come to ruin. He would not care for his own yard nor the wall of protection around it. Maintenance of his grounds and equipment would not be a priority. He would waste the resources available to him (18:9).

6. The Sluggard _____ (26:16).

Even though he has come to an obviously foolish conclusion, "lions in the street," the sluggard wants no one to try to counsel or reason with him to any different conclusion. **He is "wise in his own eyes"** and even though seven men gave him a wise answer he will not consider it.

FATHER-SON INTERACTION ACTIVITY 1

1. Look up these verses and note the rewards of the diligent worker.

REWARDS

10:4 _____

13:4 _____

14:23 _____

20:13 _____

28:19 _____

2. Look up these verses and note the consequences of being a sluggard.

CONSEQUENCES

6:11 _____

10:4 _____

12:24 _____

19:15 _____

20:4, 20:13 _____

28:19 _____

FATHER-SON INTERACTION ACTIVITY 2

1. *What does Proverbs tell us about the action of a sluggard on the job?*

_____

_____

2. *Read Proverbs 21:17a and discuss why it leads to poverty. How does this relate to the sluggard?*

_____

_____

3. *Now relate these verses to your own work ethic, whether you have a job in public or a job to do around your home or school. Do you do more talk than work? More play than work?*

Discuss areas in which you can become a more diligent worker and the consequences to you for not being diligent. Concentrate on one area of work this week on which you can improve.

_____

_____

4. Make a chart of these and other areas listing the rewards (benefits) for diligence and the consequences for laziness.

<u>DILIGENCE | LAZINESS</u>

SCHOOL WORK

_____

_____

CHORES AT HOME

_____

_____

MUSIC PRACTICE

_____

_____

EMPLOYMENT

_____

_____

FATHER-SON INTERACTION ACTIVITY 3

1. Look up Proverbs 12:27 and contrast the hunting trip of the diligent and the slothful.

_____

_____

2. Read the humorous description of the way a sluggard eats in Proverbs 19:24 and 26:15

Describe him.

_____

_____

3. What eventually would be the outcome of a slothful farmer in Proverbs 24:30-34?

Describe his vineyard.

_____

_____

4. What is the contrast between the way the slothful and the way of the righteous in Proverbs 15:19?

_____

_____

5. What do you think is the meaning of the two descriptions of the slothful messenger found in Proverbs 10:26?

_____

_____

6. Contrast the outcome of the diligent and the slothful in Proverbs 12:24.

_____

_____

Now apply these principles to your own life. Complete these projects.

PROJECT 1: *Look for some job around your house that you can do and take the initiative to do it without being asked. Which job did you complete?* _____

PROJECT 2: *Ask your father for illustrations of someone he know (no names necessary) who was fired from his job. What were the reasons? How many fit the description of the sluggard?*

_____

_____

PROJECT 3: *Review the work habits of the wise son and of the sluggard in this chapter. Ask your dad if there are any work habits in which you can improve to become a better worker. List a few.*

_____

_____

PROJECT #4: *Work with your father to develop a schedule for your time spent at home. Include sleep, getting ready, homework, recreation, eating, and other major activities. Try to discipline your time according to that schedule.*

FATHER-SON INTERACTION ACTIVITY 4

Memorize Proverbs 6:6. Quiz each other on it.

CHAPTER COMPLETION

Check here when you've completed Chapter 8.

FATHER _____ SON _____

9

Hear, My Son, About

the Forbidden Woman

My son, keep my words and treasure up my commandments with you;

to keep you from the forbidden woman, from the adulteress with her smooth words.

Proverbs 7:1,5

When a father mentions something and then spends time talking to his son on the topic repeatedly, it is obviously of great importance. In Proverbs, chapters 2 to 9, the father instructs the son in four extended passages on **perhaps the greatest danger that the son will face in his life, the danger of forbidden women.**

In Proverbs 1 and 2 the father has already instructed the son concerning evil companions. In Proverbs 2:16-19 he introduces the topic of the "forbidden woman." The father follows his introductory thoughts with longer paragraphs (5:15-21; 6:24-32: 7:1-27), where he goes into detail concerning her character, her conduct and her end. He counsels the son on the consequences of getting involved with her and on how to avoid her.

"Lady Wisdom" tells us in Proverbs 7:7 that it is the young men, the sons, who are the prey of these evil women. She further describes the targeted ones as simple youths who lack judgment. These naive young men lack experience in discerning character. They respond without reasoning and thinking through the possible consequences of their actions. For this reason the father spends considerable time giving instruction to his son concerning the forbidden woman.

THE IDENTITY OF THE FORBIDDEN WOMAN

She is described as a "forbidden woman" in these verses: Prov. 2:16, 5:3, 5:20, 6:24, 7:5. This seems to indicate that she was possibly a foreigner from another country but it is more fitting to see her as "one who is outside the circle of proper relations (with her husband), i.e., a harlot or an adulteress." She is a foreigner to a righteous husband-wife relationship.

1. *Proverbs 7:10 describes the clothes of these women. What word is used to describe her heart?*

_____

2. *Look up the definition of the word above and write it out.*

_____

_____

3."Companion" *can be translated "friend." How is the forbidden woman described in Proverbs 2:17?* _____

4. *Who do you think was the "companion of her youth" that she forsook?*

_____

THE CONDUCT OF THE FORBIDDEN WOMAN

Look up the verses and identify the missing words.

1. She is _____ and with her words _____ (2:16; 6:24; 7:5).

From the beginning of this study the father has instructed the son "to hear" him. The son was not to listen to the enticing words of sinners (1:10), but "Receive my words!" was the father's counsel.

With the father's instruction comes another warning to protect his son against the smooth talk and flattering words of the forbidden woman. She is deceitfully smooth in her words, saying things just to lure her prey into her lustful trap.

2. She is disloyal and unfaithful to her _____ and to her _____ (2:17).

She "forsakes the companion of her youth," that is, her husband. He was the guide (friend) of her youth to whom she was being unfaithful by enticing men to give up their purity for acts of physical pleasure.

She "forgets the covenant of her God." This seems to not only refer to breaking the marriage covenant that she made with her husband before God, but also the breaking of the covenant of God to his people. She is unfaithful to her God by breaking the seventh commandment.

- Write out the seventh commandment:

  _____
  _____

- Find a Bible dictionary or a regular dictionary and define "covenant."

  _____
  _____

- She lacks _____, is _____, and is _____
  _____ (7:11,12).

Described is a woman who doesn't even know where she is going. She has no discernment to see where the path of her feet are taking her. Her ways are so changeable that she has no consistent direction. Yet **she is surely on a path that will destroy her and any who takes it with her**. Proverbs 7:12 says, "At every street corner, she lies in wait." Her feet are described as abiding not at home (7:11). She is always on the go looking for her next victim.

3. She relies on _____ not _____. (6:25; 7:10)

The forbidden woman can be **identified often by her outward appearance**. She generally has some degree of beauty because the son is warned in Proverbs 6:25 against lusting after "her beauty." She fixes up the outside by making the eyes and the body more seductive. Little is said concerning the "attire of a harlot" (Proverbs 7:10), but we must assume that "immodesty" would describe it. Her eyelids may have been painted like Jezebel's face (2 Kings 9:30). There was some unnatural attraction that she brought to herself by her eyes.

4. She is _____ and _____ (7:11).

The forbidden woman can be **identified by her boisterousness**. She is loud rather than meek and quiet in spirit (1 Peter 3:4). Her rebelliousness can be seen by her lack of obedience to authority. She not only disregards her husband's authority but also the authority of her God.

5. She appears to be _____ (7:14).

She appears to be religious and **might claim a right relationship with God**. She offers very pious words to her prospective lover. She tells him, "Today I have paid my vows" (7:14). She had made her "peace offerings that day" and invites her victim to join in the feast with her. She may be using food and herself as a lure to a very sinful activity. Just because a person attends church does not mean that they are exempt from being a seducer, nor from being seduced.

6. She lures through all the senses (Proverbs 7:10-21; cf. 1 John 2:16).

Look up the verses below and fill in the "lure." Then list which sense (TOUCH, SIGHT, SMELL, HEARING, OR TASTE) to which she appealed.

LURES | SENSES

7:10 _____

7:11 _____

7:13 _____

7:14 _____

7:17 _____

THE CONSEQUENCES OF FALLING TO THE FORBIDDEN WOMAN

Look up the verses and identify the missing words.

1. He will face an untimely _____ (2:18,19; 5:11; 7:26,27)

Death in Proverbs primarily means a premature death. Just as a righteous life generally extends one's life, so an unrighteous life will shorten one's life. In Proverbs 2:18-19, 5:11, and 7:26-27, **the father is warning the son of premature death** to those who fall to the forbidden woman.

He will expose his body to many destructive sexual diseases (5:11). Anyone involved in immoral sexual sins will open himself to contacting sexually transmitted diseases that could destroy his body. Many of these can be terminal, while others shorten a person's life or cause major health problems.

2. He will come to _____ (6:26).

Proverbs 6:26 tells us the man who is seduced by the evil woman is brought to a "loaf of bread." He loses his money and possessions and is reduced in earthly value to that of a loaf of bread.

3. He will eventually have remorse over a foolish lifestyle (5:12-14).

When the naive youth comes to physical, spiritual, emotional, social, and financial poverty because of his involvement with the forbidden woman, he will usually have great remorse over the way he has lived. He will question how he could have rejected the instruction of his teachers. Proverbs 5:14 indicates a social stigma in his relationship to the righteous.

WISE COUNSEL TO THE SON

Look up the verses and identify the missing words.

1. He is to stay away from her area. (5:4)

Proverbs 5:8 instructs the son to remove his way far from her. The son should not frequent neighborhoods, places of amusement, or businesses where these woman make their appeals. Proverbs 7:25 warns to not go astray in her paths.

2. He is to make _____ and the woman in his life _____ (7:4,5).

In these verses wisdom is to be the son's sister and understanding the son's kinswoman. Two against one is always good odds! In this case it will keep the son from the strange women.

3. He is to listen to the words of his father (7:1).

Proverbs 7:1 reminds the son again to keep his father's commandments and live. He should keep them close at hand and be constantly reminded of them. The promise to the son is life, which the wise son will choose.

FATHER-SON INTERACTION ACTIVITY 1

1. There are other verses in Proverbs that describe ungodly women. Look up the verses and list each description.

DESCRIPTION

7:26 _____

11:22 _____

12:4 _____

14:1 _____

21:9 _____

22:14 _____

23:27,28 _____

25:24 _____

27:15 _____

27:16 _____

2. List the positive instruction that will keep one from the forbidden woman.

INSTRUCTION

1:10 _____

1:15 _____

1:33 _____

3:1 _____

3:7 _____

3:21 _____

4:5,6 _____

4:13 _____

4:25 _____

4:26 _____

8:32-34 _____

9:6 _____

FATHER-SON INTERACTION ACTIVITY 2

What do you think Proverbs 7:22,23 means?

_____
_____
_____

Think about these verses in relation to some Bible characters. How did each handle the temptation and what was their end? Discuss together.

1. Samson (Judges 16)

_____
_____

2. David (2 Samuel 11:1-21; 12:19; Psalm 51)

_____
_____

3. Solomon (1 Kings 11:1-13)

_____
_____

4. Joseph (Genesis 39:7-21)

_____
_____

FATHER-SON INTERACTION ACTIVITY 3

1. *Define modesty (pertaining to women's dress standards from:*

A DICTIONARY: _____

THE BIBLE: _____

2. *Describe the immodest woman.*

_____

_____

3. *Look through a women's clothing catalog and point out ladies' dresses and casual clothes of modesty and immodesty.*

4. *Fathers, the next time your family is in a large city, consider driving by the places where forbidden women do their "business." From your car, see if family members can spot them by their appearance or actions. Remind your family of the consequences to the men who fall prey to these forbidden women.*

FATHER-SON INTERACTION ACTIVITY 4

Memorize Proverbs 7:1,5. Quiz each other on it.

CHAPTER COMPLETION

Check here when you've completed Chapter 9.

FATHER ____ SON ____

Until a son understands the dangers

and benefits of dating and has

determined to select his dates based on

a certain standard, he probably isn't

ready to start dating.

10

Hear, My Son,

About the Excellent Woman

"An excellent wife who can find?

She is far more precious than jewels."

Proverbs 31:10

Most of the references to women in Proverbs speak about the snares placed in the son's path by forbidden women. We have already discussed these women in the previous chapter, examining their lifestyle and giving warnings about involvement with them. However, Proverbs 31 is included to give sons a positive alternative, to contrast the identity, character, and benefits of the excellent, or virtuous, woman.

Since the choice of a woman for his lifelong companion is probably the second greatest decision a son will make in his lifetime (the first being his choice for salvation), it is vitally important that he be given some instruction in how to find a godly wife (Proverbs 18:22). Since every girl that a guy dates is a potential marriage partner, the father and mother should start early to educate their son to discern the negative and positive qualities of each date. He should know the dangers and benefits that come with the dating opportunities. In fact, until a son understands the dangers and benefits of dating and has determined to select his dates based on a certain standard, he probably isn't ready to start dating.

Although this section of Proverbs is not written by Solomon, it is vital that we examine it. Proverbs 31:10-31 is the only extended passage in Proverbs that addresses the topic of a godly woman. It is structured and written in such a way as to be a fitting close to the entire book.

This praise to an excellent, virtuous woman is written in the form of an acrostic poem. The first letter of each verse follows the order of the Hebrew alphabet. By using an acrostic the writer is usually indicating that he is thoroughly dealing with the topic in an orderly way, just as if we were to outline a subject using A to Z. It also facilitates the memorization of the passage. Other examples of the Bible written in that manner are found in Psalm 119 and Lamentations 1-4.

A Hebrew acrostic poem in this situation contains twenty-two verses, each verse beginning with a different letter in alphabetical order. The truths and virtues of this godly woman were easier to learn and to recall because of the structure.

Use a dictionary to define the word "acrostic."

THE IDENTITY OF THE WOMAN

Look up the verses and identify the missing words.

1. She is called _____ (31:10).

The word excellent is translated virtuous in the King James Version, and means strength. She was a woman of moral strength and strength of character. Such a woman was evidently difficult to find, implied by the question, "Who can find one?" Abraham sent a servant a good distance to find a wife for Isaac (Gen. 24:3,4). The verses that follow Proverbs 31:10 presented the son with specific qualities of a godly woman. The focus is on character and conduct, not on outward beauty (31:30). The son is encouraged to focus on these qualities as he develops his list of qualities he wants in a wife.

2. Her value is _____ (31:10).

King Lemuel wants his son to see the value of finding a woman who bears these qualities, to realize that to find a virtuous woman is far better than worldly wealth. Even though rubies are of great value, contain sparkling beauty, take much time to find, and increase in value, **the godly woman is worth much more than rubies!**

3. She is an example of _____ (31:10; 18:22).

Even though the woman identified in Proverbs 31 is already married, she is an example of the kind of wife that King Lemuel's mother desired for him, and that he in turn now desires for his son. Even though the circumstances vary through which these qualities can be discerned, the son must learn to recognize virtuous character qualities in premarital life situations.

THE CHARACTER OF THE WOMAN

Look up the verses and identify the missing words.

1. She is _____ (31:11,12).

The excellent, virtuous woman can be trusted, not only with material possessions and financial responsibilities, but with her husband's confidence as well. He can confide in her and know that she will keep it to herself. **He can be transparent with her without any fear of gossip or rejection.** Her loyalty will be for life, evidenced by her consistent action of doing "him good and not evil all the days of her life" (31:12). Her loyalty and trustworthiness to her parents and others in authority over her before marriage will be a good indication of the strength of these qualities to her husband after marriage.

2. She is _____ (31:13-24).

This woman has many talents and abilities used regularly in her daily life. She has many domestic and vocational skills. Even though some of her activities would never be done in today's culture, her industry is to be admired and should be seen in the lifestyle of godly women today. *Find each verse and name the activity in which the "Excellent Woman" was involved.*

ACTIVITY

31:13,19 _____

31:14 _____

31:15 _____

31:16 _____

31:16 _____

31:22 _____

31:24 _____

3. She is _____ (31:27).

This woman is no sluggard! She is regularly up early in the morning to start her activities (31:15). She does her work with vigor and strength (31:17) and throughout her day she refuses to be idle with nothing to do (31:27). She doesn't go to bed at sundown, but works late into the night making her merchandise to sell (31:18). The wise son will realize that a woman who is lazy before marriage will be a lazy wife in marriage!

4. She is _____(31:20,26).

She is a woman who is sensitive to the needs of others. Even though she obviously comes from a higher class she does not turn a deaf ear to the poor and the needy. Her hands are ready to meet the needs of those less fortunate than she (cf. Deut. 15:7,8). Her life is controlled by a law which she readily repeats and obeys, the "law of kindness" (31:26).

5. She is _____ (31:25).

The excellent woman is clothed with positive character (31:25). Though she must have been dressed beautifully in scarlet wool, silk, and purple linen (31:21,22), she was not so concerned about outward beauty that she neglected inward character.

She may have been beautiful, as was Solomon's wife (Song of Solomon 1:15), but she certainly kept the right perspective by recognizing that "beauty is vain" (31:30), of no lasting value. Thus **she excelled in virtue, the strength of character that really makes the person and that has lasting value**. The wise son will value godly character in a prospective mate far above physical, temporal beauty. Immodest, seductive clothing belongs to the forbidden woman who puts her emphasis on outward beauty to hide her inward ugliness. The godly woman is clothed with character, radiating true inward, lasting beauty. The wise son can tell the difference.

6. She _____ (31:30).

Mentioned last is the capstone, the highest quality anyone can have. It is the character quality which forms a base for all others. **This woman "fears the Lord"** (31:30). (Review Chapter 2 on fearing the Lord.) Primary on the wise son's list in the pursuit of a godly mate must be that she "fears the Lord," for without this quality the woman is unacceptable to the godly son and to God himself (cf. II Cor. 6:14 and Eccl. 12:13).

BENEFITS TO THE GODLY WOMAN

1. She will be praised for her virtue and works (31:28-31).

Because of her virtuous life people will praise her. She will be remembered and blessed for her good works and strength of character. *Look up the verses and fill in the chart below.*

RESPONSE TO HER VIRTUE

31:11 _____

31:28 _____

31:28 _____

31:30 _____

31:31 _____

2. She will increase the influence of her husband (31:23).

Her husband was probably a judge and a highly respected member of the judicial body that met daily at the gates to determine laws. It was either her virtuous life that was above reproach which contributed to her husband's influence or her activity of good works and her positive reputation in the community that enhanced her husband's popularity. Likely it was both.

FATHER-SON INTERACTION ACTIVITY 1

1. From the following verses list the negative character traits to avoid in a woman.

NEGATIVE CHARACTERISTICS

11:22 _____

12:4 _____

19:13,27:15 _____

21:19 _____

25:24 _____

30:20 _____

2. From the following verses, list additional positive qualities of the godly woman.

POSITIVE QUALITIES

12:4 _____

14:1 _____

18:22 _____

19:14 _____

FATHER-SON INTERACTION ACTIVITY 2

First, with your father, make a list of godly character qualities that could guide you in the selection of possible future dates. List several below.

_____

_____

Next, prepare a set of dating standards including the general principles, and commit to your parents and to God that you will allow these godly standards to guide your dating life. There is an example of Dating Standards in the Appendix, page 113. Review them before each date. As Daniel purposed to keep himself pure before God (Daniel 1:8a), you, too, can purpose to have a dating life that brings glory to God.

Finally, purchase and read a Christian book on dating for teens.

FATHER-SON INTERACTION ACTIVITY 3

Memorize Proverbs 31:30. Quiz each other on it.

CHAPTER COMPLETION

Check here when you've completed Chapter 10.

FATHER ____   SON ____

My son, if your heart is wise,

my heart too will be glad.

My inmost being will exult

when your lips speak what is right.

Proverbs 23:15.16

11

Hear, My Son, About

A Controlled Tongue

My son, if your heart is wise, my heart too will be glad.

My inmost being will exult when your lips speak what is right.

Proverbs 23:15,16

Many places in Scripture God gives instructions to his people concerning the use of their tongues. The serpent lied, Eve made excuses, the children of Israel murmured, and Judas betrayed Jesus, all wrong uses of the tongue. In contrast, David sang, Daniel prayed, and Paul preached. **The tongue has the potential for both good and evil** (10:11).

In Proverbs the father thoroughly instructed his son to control his tongue and the words which he spoke. The word *tongue* is used nineteen times, *mouth* forty-eight times, *lips* forty-three times, and *words* forty times. He obviously considered what his son said, and how he said it, to be of great importance.

THE UNCONTROLLED TONGUE

For a really humorous picture of the uncontrolled tongue, read James 3:1-10!

1. The lying tongue

In about twenty-three passages or individual Proverbs, the misuse of the tongue by lying is mentioned. More than any other misuse, lying seems to predominate. In Proverbs 6:16-19 lying is listed two times in a list of seven things that the Lord hates, that are an abomination to Him. With two out of seven in this passage and one out of ten in the Ten Commandments dealing with the sin of lying, to "put away lying" (Eph. 4:25) is a priority to God and to the father. *Look up these verses and fill in the charts.*

CHARACTER OF THE LIAR

10:18 _____

12:17 _____

14:5 _____

17:4 _____

19:22 _____

25:14 _____

25:18 _____

26:28 _____

29:12 _____

THE END OF THE LIAR

12:19 _____

19:5a _____

19:5b _____

21:6 _____

21:28 _____

2. The angry tongue

There are several warnings in Proverbs concerning being an angry person and associating with people who are angry (22:24-25). The word "anger" describes an emotion that does not necessarily have to result in sinful actions (19:11), but in Proverbs the word is used to describe the sinful outbursts of the angry person (29:22). These verses show the results of anger and the benefits of controlling it. *Look up the verses and fill in the charts:*

RESULTS OF ANGER

14:17 _____

14:29 _____

19:19 _____

22:24-25 _____

29:22a _____

29:22b _____

BENEFITS OF CONTROLLING ANGER

15:1 _____

15:18 _____

3. The flattering tongue

Augustus Strong warnings against flattering speech are found in Proverbs. In four passages the father warned his son against the flattering words of a friend seeking favor of strange women. Flattery can be defined as "insincere compliments that are given with wrong motives; excessive praise for the purpose of gaining favor in someone else's eyes." The son was instructed to stay away from the flatterer (20:19) because **the flatterer "works ruin"** (26:28) and "spreads a net (trap) for his feet" (29:5). These consequences seem to apply both to the flatterer and to his victim. Either might be ensnared.

4. The gossiping tongue

Slander and gossip seem to be quite prevalent in today's society! From national politics to talk about church leaders, **people gossip and slander, destroying the person's reputation by defaming his character and embarrassing his family**. The person who is a slanderer is a "fool" (10:18). He is one who will destroy his own friendships and the friendships of others (16:28), because he reveals secrets. These will eventually get back to the one slandered, resulting in strife and broken friendships.

5. The foolish tongue

Foolishness encompasses many wrong uses of the tongue! One person may talk too much (10:19), and another may talk when he should be working (14:23). The tongue "pours out folly" (15:2) and answers before hearing all sides, bringing embarrassment to the person because of an inappropriate answer (18:13). Similarly, there is a man who is "hasty in his words" (29:20), speaking before he thinks. The commentary on him is that "there is more hope for a fool than for him!"

6. Other misused tongues

Look up these verses and list other types of uncontrolled tongues.

OTHER TYPES OF MISUSE

4:24 _____

11:9 _____

11:13 _____

15:28 _____

17:4 _____

19:28 _____

25:23 _____

27:2 _____

THE CONTROLLED TONGUE

For a beautiful hope of a genuinely controlled tongue, read Colossians 4:6.

1. A truthful tongue

For the wise son, honesty is not only "the best policy," it is the only policy! **Without honesty, genuine relationships cannot exist with God or with others**. A relationship or agreement based on a lie has a sandy foundation and cannot last. Speaking the truth must be "put on" when lying is "put off" (Eph. 4:22-25). The son with an honest tongue will have a good reputation (Proverbs 3:3,4) and will have favor in the sight of God (3:4). This son will always tell the truth (12:17) and give a correct answer (22:21).

2. An encouraging tongue

Proverbs 25:11 describes the son who knows what to say at the right time. His words are "fitly spoken," appropriate to encourage those who need it. Another verse says that "gracious words are like a honeycomb, sweetness to the soul and health to the body" (16:24). Here is the son who by his pleasant words is able to say something that ministers to the emotional and physical needs of another (12:25). Proverbs 25:25 reminds us that encouraging words written to people we know and love who are far from home are **"like cold water to a thirsty soul," a refreshing experience.**

3. A teaching tongue

Receiving and giving wise, godly counsel is encouraged throughout Proverbs. In Proverbs 27:9, "Oil and perfume make the heart glad, and the sweetness of friend comes from his earnest counsel." "In an abundance of counselors there is safety" (11:14; 24:6). Someone was certainly controlling the tongue to give wise counsel in these verses! These were wise sons! Proverbs established that teaching is a good use of the tongue when the father asked his son to hear his instructions (1:8).

4. Other controlled uses of the tongue

Look up these verses and list how the tongue may be used for good.

GOOD USES

10:19 _____

11:12 _____

11:13 _____

11:30 _____

12:18 _____

13:3 _____

15:1 _____

15:7 _____

17:9 _____

⸻

FATHER-SON INTERACTION ACTIVITY 1

Together review both the uncontrolled and the controlled uses of the tongue and each determine your strengths and your weaknesses. Choose one weakness each to work on for the next few weeks. Help each other to identify times you fail and times you succeed as you seek to keep one another accountable for better tongue control. You may even want to make a game of it: 25 cents in a jar for each infraction by the other! If you get one weakness controlled, pick another one to add and work on both. At the end of a specified time (4 to 6 weeks), use the money to go out for ice cream or steak! The more you catch each other failing, the more money there will be!

FATHER-SON INTERACTION ACTIVITY 2

Do either of you have an anger problem? Determine now to deal with it! Develop a planned response for the situation in which you most frequently respond in sinful anger. Remember that Ephesians 4:26 tells us we can have the emotion of anger, but not the sinful thoughts and actions that usually accompany it.

In order to avoid these sinful responses, however, we must plan a new response ahead of time and ask God to help us implement it when the next anger-provoking situation arises. Report to each other on progress! Get excited with each other as you get a handle on anger!

FATHER-SON INTERACTION ACTIVITY 3

Be an encourager and get into the good habit of writing notes to your family members, relatives, college students or missionaries. Remember how encouraging words from home can be (Prov. 25:25). Mark it on your calendar at certain intervals (weekly, monthly) as you schedule encouraging notes into your lifestyle. Begin now as you write your first encouraging note to someone in your immediate family. Be genuine and they'll appreciate the encouragement! It doesn't need to be long, just encouraging!

FATHER-SON INTERACTION ACTIVITY 4

Memorize Proverbs 25:11. Quiz each other on it.

CHAPTER COMPLETION

Check here when you've completed Chapter 11.

FATHER ____   SON____

12

Hear, My Son, About the Lord Jesus Christ

For whoever finds me finds life and obtains favor the LORD.

Proverbs 8:35

Throughout the first nine chapters of the book of Proverbs the son is instructed to seek after and embrace wisdom (2:4). He is told that wisdom is the principal thing (4:7) and that "the fear of the Lord is the beginning of wisdom" (9:10). Wisdom is repeatedly the topic. Its importance as a topic of instruction and as a quality to develop for a successful, meaningful life is without question. **The father realized that without wisdom his son would fall to the snares and traps in life that would destroy his effectiveness for God.**

The father used personification of wisdom to make the qualities of wisdom more personal. Personification is used often in poetry where an inanimate object or quality is described as being a person, giving life to non-life. This makes the writing more vivid and descriptive.

Wisdom in this context takes on the personal characteristics of a woman. She might be called "Lady Wisdom." She stands in marked contrast to the forbidden woman and to the foolish woman.

THE IDENTITY OF JESUS CHRIST (8:22-36)

In Proverbs 8:22-36, many question of whom the passage is speaking. Some see only the continued poetic personification of wisdom. Others see the actual person of Jesus Christ being revealed in His preincarnate existence. The preincarnate existence of Christ is describing the coexistence Christ had with God the Father throughout all eternity up to the time of his birth, i.e. his incarnation (coming in flesh). **The preincarnate revelation of Christ and his part in God's plan**

occur many times throughout Old Testament literature, and seem to be the case in this passage.

Even though the son at that time may not have understood the significance of this passage, as we reflect on the New Testament passages that allude to Proverbs 8:22-36, there is little doubt to the New Testament reader as to the person in reference.

Earlier passages in Scripture, from Genesis 3:15 in the Pentateuch, to Psalm 22 in the Poetic Books, to Isaiah 52-53 in the Prophets, reveal Christ and His part in redemption's plan. Even though the inspired writers and the reader may not have fully understood, with progressive revelation we now understand the mystery that has been revealed in Jesus Christ (1 Cor. 2:7). Augustus Strong said in *Systematic Theology* said, "There is progress in revelation from the earlier to the later books of the Bible, but this is not progress through successive steps of falsehood; it is rather progress from a less to a more clear and full unfolding of the truth."

James Buswell completes the thought by saying, "The best known and most easily traceable instance of progressive revelation is to be found in the revelation of the plan of salvation." Jesus Christ, who He is, and what part He has in the plan of salvation, is revealed here in the book of Proverbs as the wisdom of God personified.

As mentioned before, there are differing opinions on the identity of wisdom in this passage. Some continue to see only wisdom as an attitude of God throughout this section; others see Jesus Christ. Whatever the case, Irving Jensen points out that "the redemptive application of this passage must ultimately bring Christ into the picture, because there is no redemption without Christ, the Son of God, and eternal Word, Wisdom, and Power of God."

Arthur Cundall said the same thing when he wrote, "If this passage suggests that wisdom was the creative agent, the New Testament certainly gives that honor to Christ (John 1:1-3,10; Col. 1:15-17; Heb. 1:2; Rev. 3:14). In this personification of wisdom the thoughts expressed by the divinely inspired writer were so accurate that when the full revelation came through Jesus Christ, God's Son, the entire section could be lifted out and applied to Him."

COMPARE PROVERBS 8 AND NEW TESTAMENT PASSAGES

To fully answer the questions and to establish the identity of the person in Proverbs 8:22-36, compare this passage with the New Testament passages concerning Jesus Christ. One should have little difficulty in identifying wisdom personified as Jesus Christ.

Fill in the chart, writing out the parallel phrase from the New Testament that compares to the one in Proverbs.

8:22 "The Lord possessed me. . ."

John 1:1,2, John 10:30, Col. 2:2,3

_____

_____

8:22 "At the beginning. . ."

John 1:1,2, John 8:58, Rev. 1:11

_____

_____

8:22 "The first of his acts of old."

1 Peter 1:20

_____

_____

8:25 "I was brought forth. . ."

John 1:14, John 1:18, John 3:16, Col. 1:15

_____

_____

8:27-30 Various involvements in creation.

John 1:3, Col. 1:16-17, Heb. 1:2

_____

_____

8:30 "I was beside him. . ."

John 10:30, John 17:5

_____

_____

8:30 "I was daily his delight. . ."

Matt. 3:17, Matt. 17:5

_____

_____

THE APPEAL OF JESUS CHRIST (8:32-34)

Jesus' appeal is to those in whom His father delights (8:31). He delighted not in the angels, but in the "sons of men," those who are the sinners for whom Christ died.

His appeal is that they "listen" to me (8:32), "hear instruction, and be wise" (8:33). Listen and hear are the same Hebrew word and remind us of the father's appeal in Proverbs 1:8, to "hear, my son."

Review our definition of hearing that was established in Chapter 3.

The son was instructed to hear because "faith comes from hearing, and hearing through the word of Christ" (Rom. 10:17). Christ is the Word of God (John 1:1), and it is by hearkening unto Him, hearing Him, embracing Him, that He would "be wise" (8:33) and be "blessed" (8:34). The wise son in verse 34 genuinely desired to hear what was said. He was "watching daily" and "waiting," showing his patience and determination (8:34).

THE PROMISE OF JESUS CHRIST (8:35)

Jesus is offering "life" and "favor of the Lord" to those who find Him. It all depends on the result of the sinner's search for wisdom and on his hearing ability. If he searches he should have his ears ready and willing to hear and to respond in faith. Jesus' promise here reminds us of His words in John 5:24 where he said, "Whoever hears my word and believes him who sent me has eternal life." **The promise of life was His to offer because He is "the life"** (John 14:6).

Christ is offering Himself! Those who respond to Him will receive eternal life. 1 John 5:11-12 expresses this idea when John says, "Whoever has the Son has life; whoever does not have the Son of God does not have life."

THE CONSEQUENCES OF REJECTING JESUS CHRIST (8:36)

There are two actions in this verse that describe the foolish son who rejects Jesus Christ. When a person rejects Jesus he *sins against* Jesus Christ by the very refusal of His appeal. Thus the refusal exhibits that person's hate for Him. Jesus said, "All who hate me love death" (8:36).

Christ offers Himself to each son today! If you have never committed your heart to Jesus Christ, the personified wisdom of God, do it today! The consequences of rejecting Him is eternal. "Whoever does not have the Son does not have (eternal) life" (1 John 5:12), but rather "loves death" (Prov. 8:36).

FATHER-SON INTERACTION ACTIVITY 1

If you have never received Jesus Christ, consider carefully the following Scriptures, reviewing Christ's offer of eternal life. Look up each verse in Romans.

1. 3:10; 3:23 -- All men are sinners.

2. 5:12; 6:23a -- The penalty for sin is death (eternal death); separation from God.

3. 5:8a -- God loved us still in our sin.

4. 5:8b -- Christ died as our substitute.

5. 6:23b (cf. Eph. 2:8-9) -- Christ offers salvation, eternal life, as a free gift.

6. 10:9 -- Confess Jesus as Lord.

7. 10:9 -- Believe that God raised him from the dead.

8. 10:13 -- Ask God to save you.

If you will follow this outline with a genuine heart, the promise of salvation in Romans 10:13 will be YOURS!

FATHER-SON INTERACTION ACTIVITY 2

Memorize Proverbs 8:35,36. Quiz each other on it.

CHAPTER COMPLETION

Check here when you've completed Chapter 12.

FATHER ___   SON ___

Congratulations!

Appendix: Dating Standards

DATING STANDARDS OF _____

1. Dating will be a help to my spiritual life, not a hindrance.

2. There will be no physical contact unless appropriate (as in skating couples, helping a girl who has fallen, helping my date on stairs if she is wearing a long dress or high heels, and so on). I will never take advantage of any girl.

3. I will neither go anywhere that might give opportunity to do wrong nor be anywhere alone with my date.

4. I will keep all my time occupied in wholesome activities, and each date will be planned around wholesome activities.

5. I will make sure my date is a Christian and growing in the Lord, and that I am growing also.

6. I will refrain from steady dating or serious relationships until I am out of high school.

7. The purpose of my dating will be to get to know the girl better, to know how to act around girls, and to make a list of the qualities I would want in a future wife. I also hope to provide fun, wholesome activities that both my date and I will enjoy.

8. I will always dress appropriately for the occasion and the place to which I take my date.

9. I will make sure that the date is approved by Dad, and that he knows where I am going, with whom, and what time I am leaving and returning to home.

10. My dating life will always be a part of my life that I can offer to the Lord and be certain that He will accept it.

Signature _____ Date _____

Mom _____ Dad _____

About the Author

Dr. Ron Allchin is the executive director of Biblical Counseling Center in greater Chicago and northwest Indiana, a role he has held since its beginning in 1989. He received his doctorate of Ministries in Biblical Counseling from Westminster Theological Seminary and is a Fellow and board member of the Association of Certified Biblical Counselors (formerly known as NANC). He has taught, pastored, and counseled youth, adults, and couples since 1970.

Ron and his wife, Sherry, enjoy traveling to various mission locations and have had the opportunity to teach counseling in many foreign countries. They have three adult children, a foster son, and seven grandchildren.

Ron and Sherry Allchin near the Sea of Galilee.

Why Biblical Counseling Center?

Biblical counseling full of grace and truth. We walk *with* you.

Since 1989, the mission of **Biblical Counseling Center** is "Helping Churches Care for People" by connecting them to Christ's sufficient work and the wisdom of his Word.

We counsel. We train. We help.

We serve churches through helping their people receive **compassionate** biblical counseling and by equipping their own people to care through counseling training and resources.

Do you want to help your church care for people?

A certified training center, BCC has **trained thousands of students worldwide** in biblical counseling principles. We offer more than 120 hours of quality instruction designed to help churches increase their **confidence and competence in caring** for the hurting. BCC designs training **solutions for all church sizes** (50 to 7000), and we offer training to **equip leaders.** Our training helps churches **develop their own complete counseling programs**.

Do you need compassionate care?

BCC has both **male and female biblical counselors**, who meet with counselees **in person and by Skype**. Experienced counselors will listen to your situation, help you understand what God desires, and walk patiently with you as **you make progress** living your life according to God's word. Please visit BiblialCounselingCenter.org to meet our biblical counselors, watch videos, get complimentary handouts, and set up an appointment: BiblicalCounselingCenter.org

NOTES

NOTES

Made in the USA
Lexington, KY
12 December 2016